CRITICAL RACE THEORY
IN YOUR SCHOOL

CRITICAL RACE THEORY IN YOUR SCHOOL

HOW TO FIGHT BACK

DR. GEORGE S. MAURER, ED.D.

LIBERTY HILL PUBLISHING

Liberty Hill Publishing
555 Winderley Pl, Suite 225
Maitland, FL 32751
407.339.4217
www.libertyhillpublishing.com

Paperback ISBN-13: 978-1-66289-727-6
Dust Jacket ISBN-13: 978-1-66289-728-3
Ebook ISBN-13: 978-1-66289-729-0

TABLE OF CONTENTS

PREFACE

I want to thank everyone who helped me become better over the years as a craftsman and a person, even when that involved tough love. You all know who you are.

We cannot continue to send our children to Caesar for their education and be surprised when they come home as Romans.

Voddie T. Baucham, Jr.

INTRODUCTION

CRITICAL RACE THEORY (CRT) has completely infiltrated the American education system. This includes public schools, private schools, and in many cases, charter schools. Don't let anyone tell you differently. In fact, to completely avoid CRT, you may have to resort to homeschooling or attending a Private Education Association (PEA). In places like California, PEA's aren't legally considered schools and they avoid the mandates which make some parents upset.

The nation's highest education leaders support CRT. When they pretend they don't, then you know they *really* do. As a parent, you may not understand CRT, but don't feel bad because they don't want you to understand CRT. That's why you need this book.

Perhaps you've seen your children working on disturbing school assignments. Maybe during COVID you heard the teacher say alarming things during virtual classroom lectures. Maybe you weren't completely sure what you just witnessed, but your mama or papa bear senses were alerted that something is wrong and you need to investigate.

First, what is Critical Race Theory? At its core, CRT teaches children that America is completely and permanently racist. It also explains schools, government, and corporations use White supremacy and capitalism to oppress people of color. Finally, CRT says we can only be saved by Marxism and its various shades of gray, such as socialism and communism. And yes, as you read through this book, you'll learn CRT is deeply rooted in oppressor vs. oppressed Marxist philosophy.

What is Marxism? We all know the word, but it often seems American educators want to keep you in the dark on this subject as well. An excellent definition came from Henry Hazlitt in 1966 from a publication called *The Freeman: Ideas on Liberty*. Mr. Hazlitt was an American journalist from a time when American journalists weren't America-hating Marxists (seems so long ago). From Mr. Hazlitt's article titled, *Marxism in One Minute*:

> *THE WHOLE GOSPEL of Karl Marx can be summed up in a single sentence: Hate the man who is better off than you are. Never under any circumstances admit that his success may be due to his own efforts, to the productive contribution he has made to the whole community. Always attribute his success to the exploitation, the cheating, the more or less open robbery of others…This basic hatred is the heart of Marxism (p.79).*[1]

To understand your typical CRT supporter, take the intense jealousy for the upper class from your average Marxist, mix in some racially charged rhetoric, and…ta-da!…you have the modern version of a Communist revolutionary. They believe socialism can cure poverty, greed, and racism. You just need to hand over your private property, personal belongings, all your freedoms, and, of course, all your money to make it happen. Not theirs, just yours, their stuff will continue to belong to them.

In many schools, these basic ideas are already embedded in every class your child attends, and sometimes quite openly. CRT supporters say anyone who opposes CRT wants to censor true history. Meanwhile, they re-write history to be more Marxist friendly every single day. Genocide? What genocide? I don't see no stinkin' genocide.

Should we teach our children about racism in America? Yes, of course, but only when they're mature enough to handle the content. As you'll see

[1] *The Freeman 1966_2.PDF, Mises Institute.* Available at: https://mises.org/files/freeman-19662pdf

later in this book, CRT introduces very disturbing content as soon as children begin kindergarten.

Can Ethnic Studies be taught without CRT? Again, yes, of course. In fact, CRT and Ethnic Studies are NOT the same thing. To explain the dissimilarities, Ethnic Studies involves learning about the histories of minority groups, such as African Americans and Hispanic Americans. CRT adds Marxist oppressor vs. oppressed ideology into Ethnic Studies. Furthermore, CRT relentlessly focuses on the negative aspects of American history without giving credit to our nation's positive contributions to the world.

If your child takes a CRT-based Ethnic Studies class, they may believe our nation still resembles the Deep South in the 1950s. One of the seminal events leading to the 60s Civil Rights movement happened on August 28, 1955 in Mississippi. On that day, Emmett Till, a 14-year-old African American, was brutally murdered for flirting with a White woman.2 According to CRT supporters, Emmett Till-like events still happen every day. However, they lack the evidence to prove it, so every time a young African American like Michael Brown is shot by a White police officer, they begin twisting the facts of the case. We cover this event in-depth later.

CRT teaches your child one negative, repetitive theme; America is the most racist and dangerous nation in the world. In some schools, they include those ideas in every single class your child attends from Kindergarten through twelfth grade, not just Ethnic Studies, **every single class**. Even worse, CRT is often taught with completely age inappropriate content.

In an interview with the Epoch Times, a mother named Robin Steenman said her daughter never identified anyone by race in her entire life. Then she attended one CRT class session and suddenly began saying

---

² *Emmett Till is murdered | August 28, 1955*, History.com. Available at: <u>https://www.history.com/this-day-in-history/the-death-of-emmett-till</u>

things like, "That Black girl," or "That White boy." In response, Ms. Steenman founded Moms For Liberty.3

Ms. Steenman and other parents begin researching the CRT content in their children's curricula (curricula is the plural version of curriculum). While reading through the lessons, the constant focus on the worst examples of American history soon caused many parents to feel depressed. If a school's CRT program can depress an adult, just imagine what it can do to your child. We learn more about Ms. Steenman and Moms For Liberty in Chapter Four.

The bad news is your child's school has most likely already entrenched CRT into their curricula. And yes, they're probably lying to you about it. The good news is I'm going to teach you to recognize it and how to fight back.

Throughout this book, you'll see Primary Lesson Tips. They provide guidance for you to follow if you recognize CRT in your children's school. You'll see some tips repeated more than once. That's because school officials pushing CRT tend to follow similar playbooks. We'll explore one such playbook in Chapter Eight.

If you're new to CRT, this book contains a lot of new information for you, but don't get overwhelmed trying to remember everything. Actually, just a handful of key words and phrases will help you recognize CRT, including *marginalization, oppression, systemic racism, White supremacy,* and *social justice.* They're repeated many times in this book, and by the end you'll remember everything you need to know.

Additionally, in this book, I am not claiming racism doesn't exist in our nation. In a country with 336+ million people (as of January 2024),[4]

---

[3] *Kids are being propagandized with racism under critical race theory-interview with Robin Steenman* | July 09, 2021, *EpochTV.* Available at: https://www.theepochtimes.com/kids-are-being-propagandized-with-racism-under-critical-race-theory-interview-with-robin-steenman_3895000.html

[4] *U.S. and World Population Clock, United States Census Bureau.* Available at: https://www.census.gov/popclock/

you'll always have plenty of bad actors. However, the facts don't support the existence of the levels of racism claimed by CRT supporters. If anything, in my opinion, CRT proponents are the worst perpetrators of racism in the country. You'll see plenty of evidence of that in this book.

Finally, for eBook readers, I chose to use *footnotes* instead of *endnotes* for my references. *Endnote* references appear all together at the end of the book, while *footnotes* appear at the bottom of each page where the reference is located. I encourage you to check out my references for yourself, especially the videos. Hyperlinks located at the bottom of each page in *Footnotes* make this more convenient for you. For print readers and audiobook listeners who also want to watch the reference videos, etc., I've posted a PDF with the hyperlinks on my Facebook group titled, *Dr. George S. Maurer, Ed.D., author.* Please join my group for the latest updates.

One more thing, thank you for reading my very first book. I am forever grateful.

CHAPTER ONE

YES, THEY'RE LYING TO YOU

Riverside Unified Schools in California (RUSD)

"RIVERSIDE UNIFIED SCHOOL District does not teach Critical Race Theory." Those were the words of Rene Hill, RUSD School Superintendent, to parents during a Board of Education meeting in Riverside, California on July 15, 2021. You can find her comments on YouTube (at the 02:59:30 mark; hyperlink provided below).[5]

Tom Hunt, RUSD School Board President, repeated that assertion later in the meeting (at the 03:17:10 mark) after another parent made a comment about CRT. If you take the time to watch the video, in my opinion, he said it with a bit of a snotty tone as well. Mr. Hunt said:

> We are not teaching CRT. We had a resolution last year. This is not what the Board elected to do.

Meanwhile, a third CRT denial from RUSD occurred a few weeks later during a Board meeting in August. Mr. Hunt again told parents rumors of CRT in Riverside schools were false. Speaking to one parent in the audience (at the 06:41:15 mark in a YouTube video; hyperlink provided

---

[5] *Live stream: RUSD board meeting 7-15-2021* (2021) *YouTube.* Available at: https://www.youtube.com/watch?v=LQvufSKKsY0

below),[6] Mr. Hunt said, *"Ma'am, I assure you…we are not teaching Critical Race Theory."* He also called the rumors *"fake news."*

However, problems arise with Ms. Hill's and Mr. Hunt's CRT denials when we revisit RUSD's school board meeting one year earlier on September 15, 2020. During that meeting, the school board voted unanimously for an ethnic studies class requirement for all Riverside high school graduates by the 2024-25 school year.[7] Also, during that meeting, the RUSD School Board gave a PowerPoint presentation explaining the newly required Ethnic Studies program.

The presentation outlined twenty-seven online learning modules included in the classes. Four lesson modules contained the words "Critical Race Theory" right in their titles. Examples include *Exploring the Permanence of Racism through Critical Race Theory, Exploring Whiteness as Property through Critical Race Theory, Exploring Interest Convergence through Critical Race Theory,* and *Exploring the Critique of Liberalism through Critical Race Theory.* In addition, eleven other modules referenced CRT-related concepts, such as *microaggressions, implicit bias,* and *systemic oppression.*[8] The final count…fifteen out of twenty-seven learning modules contain CRT.

Let's take a moment to further explain a few of these terms. *Microaggressions* are subtle slights and snubs that occur during interactions between people of different races and cultures. An example might be when a White man speaks to a mixed-race group, he only speaks directly to other White people or he greeted the people of color last. *Implicit bias* is unconscious racism that creates assumptions about people of other races.

---

[6] Live stream: RUSD board meeting 8-5-2021 (2021) YouTube. Available at: https://www.youtube.com/watch?v=59axVpZZLzk

[7] Yarbrough, B. (2020) *Riverside Unified Makes Ethnic Studies a graduation requirement,* Press Enterprise. Available at: https://www.pressenterprise.com/2020/09/18/riverside-unified-makes-ethnic-studies-a-graduation-requirement/

[8] Meetings: Equity & Access Updates: Growing Our Equity Culture, RUSD Board of Education (2021) eBOARDsolutions. Available at: https://simbli.eboardsolutions.com/Meetings/Attachment.aspx?S=36030406&AID=63188&MID=3881

An example might be the White store clerk who watches African American customers more closely than White customers. *Systemic oppression*, defined by CRT as *systemic racism*, occurs at the institutional level of organizations. An example might be that American schools design classes to make White children succeed and African American students fail.

To further explain, White and Asian students perform better in schools than African American, Indigenous, and Hispanic students. This is called the *Achievement Gap*. Through the lens of CRT and systemic oppression, the achievement gap exists because schools purposefully design classes for students of color to fail. At the same time, they're designed to help White and Asian students to excel. If you're confused by this concept, don't worry. It confuses me as well.

Returning to RUSD's School Board meetings, during the September 15th get-together (at the 01:31:20 mark on YouTube; hyperlink provided below), Ms. Hill said the district supported including Ethnic Studies perspectives (code for CRT) in all areas of the RUSD curriculum, including math and science. Essentially, CRT in every single class. **Every single class.** CRT was never intended to be one single course. It's designed to change your child's entire education.[9]

To review the facts, in 2021, Ms. Hill and Mr. Hunt completely denied CRT in RUSD's Ethnic Studies program. Yet, in 2020 they vote unanimously to pass the Ethnic Studies program and described classes which contained CRT in more than half of its learning objectives. It just doesn't add up, so I reached out to RUSD in August 2023 to get further clarification. The email I received back said:

> *Critical Race Theory is not part of the Riverside Unified School*
> *District's curriculum. All academic work is based on the State of*

---

[9] *Live stream: RUSD board meeting 9-15-2020 (2020) YouTube. Available at:* https://www.youtube.com/watch?v=Ml1AJ7AhC7I

*California Content Standards. Please find RUSD's History and
Social Science webpage to review the Ethnic Studies information.*

First, I'm pretty sure that's the standard response they send to everyone
who asks about CRT. Second, I feel sorry for the poor Public Information
Officer (PIO) who has to send this stuff out. I strongly suspect he or she
knows their information is incorrect, at least at some level. Intentionally
deceiving others always comes with a price.

Just for fun, let's unpack RUSD's official response. *CRT is not part
of RUSD's curriculum.* We know that information is incorrect because
RUSD's 2020 Ethnic Studies PowerPoint presentation says fifteen out of
twenty-seven learning objectives contain CRT.

Let's look at sentence #2. *All academic work is based on the State of
California Content Standards.*[10] I assume this refers to California's Ethnic
Studies Model Curriculum (CESMC). For those outside the Golden
State, it took four versions to get final approval for CESMC. The first ver-
sion was so extreme, it used *hxrstory* instead of history in many places. I'll
explain *hxrstory*, or H-X-R-story, later in the book. Even after four updates,
the CESMC is still wall-to-wall CRT. They simply removed the words
"Critical Race Theory," but left behind all the concepts. This is something
see this over and over as you go through the book. More on CESMC in
Chapter Three.

On to sentence #3. *Please find RUSD's History and Social Science webpage to review the Ethnic Studies information.*[11] In fact, I did find RUSD's
History and Social Science webpage and I reviewed the Ethnic Studies
information. Much like CESMC, I did not find the words "Critical Race

---

[10] *Ethnic studies model curriculum, Ethnic Studies Model Curriculum–Curriculum Frameworks
& Instructional Materials (CA Dept of Education).* Available at: https://www.cde.ca.gov/
ci/cr/cf/esmc.asp

[11] *RUSD history social science–ethnic studies, RUSD History Social Science–Ethnic Studies.*
Available at: https://sites.google.com/riversideunified.org/rusdhistorysocialscience/
ethnic-studies?authuser=0

Theory," but I did find its concepts embedded throughout the program. From the first paragraph of the webpage:

> When we elevate and recognize the histories and identities of marginalized groups, we create powerful opportunities for students to see their stories as part of the fabric of United States history. In doing so, we empower students to engage in civic action to improve our nation for all citizens.

This paragraph is typical of CRT-infused course descriptions. We often see strongly-worded optimistic ideas which seem to indicate positive learning objectives. However, the CRT code words *marginalized groups* reveal the true nature of the class and you can expect a large focus on oppressor vs oppressed themes. As someone who educated himself on CRT, I interpret this paragraph in the following manner: *We seek positive outcomes for students using racial divisions and shaming them for historical atrocities.* Hard to get positive outcomes by shaming and dividing students.

The RUSD webpage further explains their Ethnic Studies program was designed to be *"an anti-racist, robust, interdisciplinary and vertically-aligned Ethnic Studies program..."* Now, let's translate these CRT code words into English. In that quote, we see the terms *anti-racist* and *vertically-aligned* Ethnic Studies program. HINT: Anti-racists are not racist like Antifascists aren't fascist. I don't want to ruin the surprise, but in this book you'll see anti-racists say some of the most racist things you've ever heard.

Now let's define the term *"vertically-aligned Ethnic Studies program."* *Study.com* defines a vertically-aligned curriculum as one where "teachers of various grades team up along a single subject."[12] You probably recognize this with English and Math classes, among others. In high school, you take Algebra, then Geometry, then Algebra II, etc. As a Freshman, you take

---

12 *Horizontally and Vertically Aligning Curriculum, Study.com.* Available at: https://study. com/academy/lesson/horizontally-and-vertically-aligning-curriculum.html

English 1. As a sophomore, you take English II, etc. Likewise, at least in California, Ethnic Studies is a multi-year, long-term curriculum. Each year builds upon previous work.

According to RUSD's Ethnic Studies webpage, the school district offers three versions of Ethnic Studies. They are *Ethnic Diversity in America*, *African American Studies*, and *Chicano Studies*. They include study units with titles such as *The Legacy of Disenfranchised and Marginalized People*; *Identity, Controversy and the Counter-Narrative*; and *The Great Depression: From Open Arms to Closed Doors*.

Marginalized people and counter-narratives come straight from CRT principles which we cover more in Chapter Two. The last unit title, *The Great Depression: From Open Arms to Closed Doors*, comes from RUSD's Chicano studies program. It sounds like the classes teach students that the Great Depression was more of a racist event and less of an economic one.

To review, in checking RUSD's History and Social Science webpage, we find plenty of CRT where RUSD claims none exists. If you remember, those denials came from official correspondence and school board meetings. One other interesting thing about the school board meetings. There seemed to be a number of participants who supported CRT. Which leads to this question. Why did they express their support for CRT when RUSD claims it doesn't teach it?

I first heard the term *seminar callers* on the Rush Limbaugh radio show. To further explain, Leftist activists regularly called Mr. Limbaugh's radio show pretending to be average citizens. During their calls, the Leftists tried to portray extremist ideas as normal hoping the conservative audience would compromise their principles slowly over time. They were obviously well organized and often used similar talking points.

Mr. Limbaugh soon recognized this trend and identified them as *seminar callers*. When he began calling out the existence of *seminar callers*, his critics called him crazy for entertaining such an idea. They claimed *seminar callers* just existed in Mr. Limbaugh's imagination. However, the truth always comes out. In 2019, using a Freedom of Information Act (FOIA) request, *The Washington Free Beacon* found documents in the Clinton Presidential Library proving the Democratic National Committee (DNC) created such a program in 1996. According to the documents, the DNC launched the *Talk Radio Initiative* (it had a name and everything) with the support of the Clinton Administration. From *The Washington Free Beacon* article:[13]

> *The program trained thousands of operatives to call in to radio shows, conduct surveillance of their contents, and secretly dissemi-nate Democratic talking points while posing as ordinary listeners. Volunteers must be able to keep the project confidential so as not to create the image of a 'Democratic conspiracy...'*

The article also interviewed a talk radio host from the Pacific Northwest named Lars Larson. Early on, Mr. Larson recognized an odd pattern just like Mr. Limbaugh:

> *You would get calls, an hour apart, from different people with dif-ferent voices and different names, but they would talk the same lines. So close that you knew that this was not a coincidence...it was the same language on the same subject and the same arguments.*

In other words, they were delivering DNC talking points verbatim. Fortunately, for you and me, the Talk Radio Initiative strategists and their seminar callers weren't smart enough to change things up a bit.

---

[13] Kakutani, Y. (2019) *Dems secretly trained thousands of activists to manipulate media, Clinton Library Docs Show, Washington Free Beacon*. Available at: https://freebeacon. com/politics/dems-secretly-fielded-thousands-of-activists-to-manipulate-media-clinton-library-docs-show/

While doing research for this book, I returned to the RUSD School Board meeting videos a number of times. I watched the meeting videos and noticed participants with similar talking points. They all supported CRT despite the fact that RUSD doesn't teach CRT. Were they seminar participants? Perhaps, but with one major difference. Before speaking, they openly identified themselves as speaking for left-leaning organizations, such as the NAACP, the BLU Educational Foundation, Anti-Racist Riverside, Stand Up Riverside, and the Center Against Racism and Trauma (CART). You can accurately guess the intended purpose of each of the aforementioned organizations. But I do give them credit for one thing, they weren't pretending to be average citizens while acting as professional social justice warriors like Mr. Limbaugh's and Mr. Larson's callers.

PRIMARY LESSONS: (1) Read the online curriculum content behind your child's classes. (2) If you run into a CRT supporter at a school board meeting, find out whom he or she represents.

Education Secretary on The View

Dr. Miguel Cardona, U.S. Secretary of Education, appeared on the television program, *The View*, on March 26, 2021. Dr. Cardona's appearance was documented on YouTube. As a broadcast professional with more than 35 years of experience, an exchange took place which appeared to me as set up and rehearsed. Here is that exchange (at the 05:13 mark, hyperlink provided below):[14]

> *View Host:* Is Critical Race Theory, as it's being bandied about right now, taught in K through 12?

---

[14] *Miguel Cardona discusses future of Education, critical race theory, mental health | the View (2021) YouTube. Available at: https://www.youtube.com/watch?v=8oOD8xlV8yY&t=319s*

Dr. Cardona: No.

View Host: Say that again please.....one more time.

Dr. Cardona: It's not.

View Host: It's not.

Different View Host: Critical Race Theory is not taught K through 12. Let me say...I can say it in Spanish too if you need...

View Host: Is it taught anywhere at any age?

Dr. Cardona: I think Law School.....

View Host: Law School.

Different View Host: Thank you for clearing that up.

Dr. Cardona *thinks* Law School. If you choose to watch the video, you may notice Dr. Cardona looks down and away when giving these answers. I'm no body language expert, but when someone looks down and away when talking to me, I feel they aren't being completely honest.

And less than one month later, look what I found. On April 19, 2021, the Department of Education (DOE) announced a new $5.3 million dollar grant program called *American History and Civics Education* for elementary and secondary education (K-12).[15] The new program is, surprise-surprise, chock full o' CRT. The grant program's first priority was to fund projects that "*incorporate racially, ethnically, culturally, and linguistically diverse*

---

[15] *Federal Register/Vol. 86, no. 73/Monday, April 19, 2021 ... Available at: https://www. govinfo.gov/content/pkg/FR-2021-04-19/pdf/2021-08068.pdf*

perspectives." To support these perspectives, the program identified an *"ongoing national reckoning with systemic racism.*"

Various versions of systemic racism are often listed as the very first CRT tenet by CRT scholars (more on this in Chapter Two where we take a deep dive into CRT concepts). Now, in order to win a grant under this program, candidates are required to consider *"systemic marginalization"* and *"biases"* in their applications. Did you pick up the CRT code words there? To review, at the time Dr. Cardona denied CRT existed in K-12 schools, he was overseeing the final details of a new grant program deeply embedded with CRT principles.

Additionally, before becoming the U.S. Secretary of Education, Dr. Cardona was Connecticut's Commissioner of Education. One of Dr. Cardona's last efforts before leaving for Washington DC was pushing through an education policy titled, *An Act Concerning the Inclusion of African American and Latino Studies in the Public School Curriculum.* Dr. Cardona's name is listed near the very top of acknowledgements.[16]

While the words "Critical Race Theory" don't appear in this education policy, CRT concepts litter the course curriculum. Almost every single course includes learning objectives such as *privilege, resistance,* and *race as a social construct. Race as a social construct* is a word-for-word tenet of CRT.

The main point here is that Dr. Cardona created an ethnic studies curriculum full of CRT principles in Connecticut. Then, he became the nation's #1 educator as Secretary of Education and began creating CRT-based programs at the U.S. Department of Education. Next, he went on *The View* and claimed American schools do not teach CRT and he thinks it might be taught in Law School. To steal the laziest line in comedy, you just can't make this stuff up.

I tried reaching out to Dr. Cardona to get his thoughts on this obvious discrepancy. Without boring you with the details, all advertised methods

---

[16] Connecticut Public Act No. 19-12, An Act Concerning the Inclusion of Black and Latino Studies in the Public School Curriculum. Available at: https://pa1912.serc.co/

to contact Dr. Cardona on *whitehouse.gov* and *ed.gov* were dead ends. Even the Education Department Press Office, which advertises itself as a way for "reporters and education writers" to reach out to Dr. Cardona, turned up nothing. Big surprise.

PRIMARY LESSON: Learn CRT principles well enough to recognize them even when the words "Critical Race Theory" have been removed. To help you, Chapter Two offers a deep dive into CRT principles.

The National Education Association

Another example of alleged CRT dishonesty comes from the *National Education Association* (NEA). In June 2021, NEA, the nation's largest teachers' union, officially adopted a policy of protecting the integrity of CRT. And here we are again. If CRT is not taught in American schools, why the need for an official policy to safeguard it? During their 2021 national conference, NEA declared CRT as a "reasonable" and "appropriate" charter for understanding the role of racism in American history. They also committed almost $128,000 to fund its defense.

Soon afterwards, the NEA quickly began covering their tracks. When the NEA national convention ended, their plan to defend CRT was still on their website. But, according to the Epoch Times, four days later, those details had been removed.[17] However, nothing is ever truly deleted on the internet. According to a Wayback Machine archive of the NEA website, the official name of the NEA's CRT defense proposal was *New Business Item 39*. Included in CRT's defense efforts, *New Business Item 39* committed

---

[17] Pan, B. (2021) *Largest Teachers' Union quietly removes pro-CRT agenda items from website*, The Epoch Times. Available at: https://www.theepochtimes.com/largest-teachers-union-quietly-removes-pro-crt-agenda-items-from-website_3890683.html

NEA President Becky Pringle to make numerous public statements supporting CRT programs across the country.[18]

One interesting side note, that particular convention featured a number of conflicting CRT messages. Randi Weingarten, President of the American Federation of Teachers (AFT), spoke to NEA attendees and denied CRT at the same convention where the NEA announced plans and committed money to defend CRT. Again, why defend something that doesn't exist? In her CRT denial comments, Ms. Weingarten said:

> *Let's be clear: critical race theory is not taught in elementary schools or high schools. It's a method of examination taught in law school and college that helps analyze whether systemic racism exists—and, in particular, whether it has an effect on law and public policy. But culture warriors are labeling any discussion of race, racism or discrimination as CRT to try to make it toxic. They are bullying teachers and trying to stop us from teaching students accurate history.*[19]

On September 02, 2023, I submitted a press inquiry from the AFT website to ask Ms. Weingarten to clarify her CRT comments. Their Contact page said the AFT welcomed emails, but for a more timely response, fill out the embedded form on the website.[20] Two months later, I was still waiting for a response. As you progress through this book, you'll learn non-responses are a common occurrence when people ask questions about CRT.

---

[18] *New business item 39, 2021 NEA Annual Meeting.* Available at: https://web.archive.org/web/20210705234008/https:/ra.nea.org/business-item/2021-nbi-039/

[19] AFT Union (2022) *A safe and welcoming school year for all,* American Federation of Teachers. Available at: https://www.aft.org/press/speeches/safe-and-welcoming-school-year-all

[20] *Contact,* American Federation of Teachers. Available at: https://www.aft.org/contact

I also sent an email to the NEA Media Center. I won't bore you with every single email I sent out while writing this book, but I'm including this email to give you an example of my inquiries. Plus, I'm really, really proud of that email. Here's the copy from that email:

Hi,

I'm an independent author writing a book about Critical Race Theory (CRT). During the 2021 NEA national convention, New Business Item 39 called for the creation of a CRT defense fund. Also, during this conference, NEA declared CRT as a "reasonable" and "appropriate" charter for understanding the role of racism in American history. New Business Item 39 also committed President Pringle to openly support CRT during her public speaking events.

During the same conference, the NEA invited Randi Weingarten, President of the American Federation of Teachers (AFT), to speak and she denied the existence of CRT in American schools.

My questions are:

Why invite Ms. Weingarten to speak and deny CRT at the same event where the NEA was launching a program to defend CRT?

Does New Business Item 39 still exist today?

If so, what name does it go by?

Why was New Business Item 39 removed from your website?

Is it NEA policy to give all business items at your national confer-
ences such benign names?

Thank you so much for your time. Please read the below excerpt
from my book on this topic (I always cut and paste the relevant
passage below my signature block, so they can see what I'm
writing about them).

Warmest regards,

george

Yes, I sign all emails to CRT supporters with "Warmest regards" and
chuckle to myself each time I do it.

PRIMARY LESSON: Be polite to school officials even when they are
obviously lying to you. If you lose your temper, you may say something
they can use against you and the entire anti-CRT movement. Keep in mind,
they are very good at telling half-truths and playing the victim.

National School Boards Association (NSBA)

Speaking of telling half-truths and playing the victim, during the pandemic, many children attended school from home using computers. As a
result, parents experienced their children's classwork firsthand, and many
were shocked at the content to which their children were exposed. When
parents began asking questions, they were often ignored or given flat out
denials of CRT in lesson plans. A little basic research often revealed those
denials were, shall we say, disingenuous.

Understandably, some parents became very upset. How would you feel
if your child's school official looked you in the eye and seemingly lied to

you? To confront these officials, parents attended school board meetings where many administrators stuck to their denials.

In school districts across the nation, parents' frustrations grew, and their complaints grew more impassioned. After all, they were defending their children. And remember, they were also angry with COVID policies and mask mandates. During the summer of 2021, while reporting about Rapid City, South Dakota school board meetings, the Associated Press (AP) reported normally dull meetings were war zones. Of course, AP firmly blamed parents for the conflicts and almost always remembered to point out in their news stories that CRT was not part of the school curriculum.[21]

On September 29, 2021, the NSBA wrote a letter to the President of the United States requesting federal assistance with threats from parents regarding CRT, COVID school lockdowns, and mask mandates. In the letter, the NSBA claimed school board officials received physical violence threats related to *"propaganda purporting the false inclusion of critical race theory within classroom instruction and curricula."*[22] While detailing threats of violence against these gentle and benevolent school board members, you may have noticed the NSBA made sure to deny CRT in classrooms.

When this story first came out, the NSBA posted the letter on their website and most news stories provided a hyperlink for people to read it firsthand.[23] Two years later, the hyperlink now defaults to a *404 Page Not Found Error.* This means they took the letter down. Since nothing is truly

---

[21] Groves, S. (2023) *Tears, politics and money: School boards become battle zones,* AP News. Available at: https://apnews.com/article/health-education-coronavirus-pandemic-school-boards-e41350b7d9e3662d279c2dad287f7009

[22] *Full NSBA letter to Biden Administration and Department of Justice memo* (2022) Parents Defending Education. Available at: https://defendinged.org/press-releases/full-nsba-letter-to-biden-administration-and-department-of-justice-memo/

[23] *NSBA-letter-to-president-biden-concerning-threats-to-public ...* Available at: https://nsba.org/-/media/NSBA/File/nsba-letter-to-president-biden-concerning-threats-to-public-schools-and-school-board-members-92921.pdf

deleted on the internet, we now must find the letter on the website of an organization called, *Parents Defending Education*.[24]

Let's explore the NSBA document to learn why they may have removed it from their website. The letter says:

> As these acts of malice, violence, and threats against public school officials have increased, the classification of these heinous actions could be the equivalent to a form of domestic terrorism and hate crimes…NSBA requests…appropriate enforceable actions against these crimes and acts of violence under the Gun-Free School Zones Act, the PATRIOT Act in regards to domestic terrorism, (the letter then goes on to list several other laws)…

In the days following the release of the letter, social media platforms were abuzz with posts about the NSBA calling parents *terrorists*. Also, the *National Review* published a news story which backed up the claim. The article was titled, *School-Board Group Asks Biden to Review Whether Parent Confrontations over CRT Constitute 'Domestic Terrorism.'*[25] Fox News published a softer version of the story without the word "terrorism" in the headline titled, *School Board Group Asks Biden to Use the PATRIOT Act Against Parents over Opposition to COVID Measures, CRT.*[26]

---

[24] *Full NSBA letter to Biden Administration and Department of Justice memo* (2022a) Parents Defending Education. Available at: https://defendinged.org/press-releases/full-nsba-letter-to-biden-administration-and-department-of-justice-memo/

[25] Downey, C. (2021) *School-Board Group asks Biden to review whether parent confrontations over CRT constitute 'domestic terrorism'*, National Review. Available at: https://www.nationalreview.com/news/school-board-group-asks-biden-to-review-whether-parent-confrontations-over-crt-constitute-domestic-terrorism/

[26] Casiano, L. and Fox News (2021) *School Board Group asks Biden to use the Patriot Act against parents over opposition to Covid measures, CRT*, Fox News. Available at: https://www.foxnews.com/politics/school-biden-threats-covid-crt-patriot-act

Shortly afterwards, the usual suspects began defending the NSBA and denied they called school parents terrorists. Let's examine AP's *fact check* on the subject:

> CLAIM: *The National School Boards Association is asking the Biden administration to label parents who protest school policies domestic terrorists.*

> AP'S ASSESSMENT: *False. The organization — the NSBA, for short — is not asking Biden to label parents who protest at school board meetings as terrorists. The NSBA asked the administration to do an interagency investigation of threats of violence against school board members and said the threats "could be the equivalent to a form of domestic terrorism and hate crimes." Biden has yet to publicly comment on the issue, and there's no indication he or the Department of Justice has called protesting parents "domestic terrorists," despite false claims to that effect by social media users.*[27]

This is the crap "fact checkers" pull all the time. Notice how the AP worded the claim. Did the NSBA's letter specifically call parents "domestic terrorists" or ask the Biden administration to label them as "domestic terrorists?" No. The AP fact checkers knew this and worded the claim so they could produce a "false" assessment and make critics of the letter appear to be lying. Technically, there was no call to label parents as terrorists.

However, did the letter compare parents' actions to terrorist acts and hate crimes? Absolutely. Did the letter ask the President to consider using the PATRIOT Act against parents *"in regards to domestic terrorism?"* Absolutely. Remember, the PATRIOT Act was specifically designed to

---

[27] Posts Mischaracterize School Board organization's letter to Biden (2023) AP News. Available at: https://apnews.com/article/fact-checking-634580066208?utm_medium=APFactCheck&utm_campaign=SocialFlow&utm_source=Twitter

expand legal investigative authority against terrorists.[28] So why would the NSBA bring up the PATRIOT Act in their letter to President?

In response, United States Attorney General (USAG) Merrick Garland announced the Federal Bureau of Investigations (FBI) would lead all investigations into threats against school officials.[29] Guess who investigates all terrorist incidents in the United States? The Attorney General primarily uses the FBI. [30] Again, the laziest line in comedy, you can't make this stuff up. Well, you could but no one would believe you.

If we return to the NSBA's letter, exactly what possible acts of domestic terror and hate crimes were outlined? The letter speaks generally of threats received through the U.S. Postal Service, social media, and in-person. It also says school board meetings in several states have been interrupted or ended by "angry mobs," but let's get more specific. The letter identified one individual in Illinois arrested for aggravated battery and disorderly conduct. In Michigan, one individual gave a Nazi salute to the school board. I assume he or she was calling the school officials "Nazis."

In Virginia, the letter identifies three people. One was arrested for an unnamed crime. The second was ticketed for trespassing. The third was hurt during a school board meeting discussion with no further explanation of the injury's cause. And in Alabama, one resident used Facebook Live to record conversations with school officials. Apparently, that's a major no-no.

The worst example comes from Ohio were someone mailed a letter to a school board member saying, *"We are coming after you and all the members on the ... BoE* [Board of Education]." Remember an earlier PRIMARY

[28] *The USA PATRIOT Act: Preserving Life and liberty.* Available at: https://www.justice.gov/archive/ll/what_is_the_patriot_act.pdf

[29] Chamberlain, S. (2021) *Garland calls in FBI to counter reported threats against school staffers,* New York Post. Available at: https://nypost.com/2021/10/05/merrick-garland-calls-in-fbi-to-counter-threats-against-school-staffers/

[30] *Terrorism incident law enforcement and investigation annex.* Available at: https://www.fema.gov/sites/default/files/2020-07/fema_incident-annex_terrorism-law-enforcement.pdf

LESSON, be polite to school officials even when they are obviously lying to you and don't lose your temper. They are very good at telling half-truths and playing the victim.

In my opinion, each of these parent's actions was most likely provoked by school officials with condescending comments or by ignoring their questions. And these parents certainly lost their tempers and crossed a line, especially the Ohio parent who told school officials he was coming after them. However, can we truly define any of these examples as terrorism? I don't think so, but obviously Attorney General Garland does. Consider this. If these parents were social justice warriors and the school administrators were defending conservative values, would the NSBA compare their actions to terrorism? Also, would Attorney General Garland declare the FBI will investigate such cases moving forward? I think we all know the answers are, "No."

In September 2023, I sent an email to the NSBA requesting a comment on their letter to the President. Signed "warmest regards," of course. You might be surprised to learn I'm still waiting for a response.

PRIMARY LESSON: Again, be polite to school officials even when they're obviously lying to you and don't lose your temper, or you may find yourself being investigated by the FBI under the PATRIOT Act as a domestic terrorist. I can't believe I just typed those words. The level of crazy in our society right now is off the charts!

Tustin Unified Schools in California

In 2021, a group of parents in Tustin, California discovered their children were given a homework assignment called *White Savior Complex* in a high school English class. They recognized elements of CRT and began asking questions. According to a *YouTube* video from *Let's Roll America*, an independent news site,[31] at the 00:20 mark in the video, Tustin Unified School District (TUSD) administrators first assured parents that CRT was not taught in Tustin schools. There's that CRT denial again. Then, at the 02:08 mark in the video, administrators said the *White Savior Complex* homework was an unauthorized assignment by a substitute teacher and TUSD will no longer use that substitute teacher. The letter then concluded with an admission of guilt by the district.

To explain the *White Savior Complex* assignment, it included something called *White Saviorism. Health.com* describes White Saviorism as the belief that White people only help people of color when it's in their own interests.[32] Sounds exactly like the CRT principle of *interest convergence,* which says White people only promote the interests of people of color when they also align with White interests.

Not satisfied with TUSD's explanation, Tustin parent, Syndie Ly, submitted five public records requests demanding all materials and communications related to Ethnic Studies from TUSD elected officials. On June 02, 2021, parents received files which proved school officials had been dishonest with them. Big surprise, right? Two weeks later, Ms. Ly challenged the Tustin School Board with her findings as documented by another YouTube video.

You may remember, TUSD firmly maintained the *White Savior Complex* assignment had been unauthorized in Tustin's schools. However, an email showed TUSD Superintendent Gregory Franklin reviewed and approved the *White Savior Complex* assignment. However, in his defense, he did express concerns about teaching it in an English class, which is where the substitute taught it. Mr. Franklin's email read, *"I took a look at the white*

[31] *Tustin USD mom Syndie Ly in the fight of her life against critical race theory and the School Board* (2021) YouTube. Available at: https://www.youtube.com/watch?v=DBMregtRv-U

[32] Murphy, C. (2023) *White Savior Complex is a harmful approach to providing help-here's why, Health.* Available at: https://www.health.com/mind-body/health-diversity-inclusion/white-savior-complex

*savior assignment…I think it's a good assignment in the ethnic studies course …
not so sure about a high school English course."*[33] We learned two things here.
First, Mr. Franklin approved a school assignment which obviously included
CRT. If he didn't recognize it, he should have. Second, TUSD lied when it
defined the assignment as "unauthorized." Mr. Franklin definitely authorized it for Ethnic Studies and the denial would've been stronger if he said,
"no," to English rather than "not so sure."

The public records request also included a second troubling email.
This one from School Board member Allyson Damikolas, who admitted
Tustin's Ethnic Studies did include CRT, so she wanted to change the
course description to create *plausible deniability* toward parents. This must
be a familiar strategy to you by now. Remove the words "Critical Race
Theory," keep the CRT content, and everything will be fine. From Ms.
Damikolas's email:

> *I had a comment on the ethnic studies presentation, the second
> bullet saying that 'it is not aligned with CRT' is slightly inaccu-
> rate in my opinion. I think it would be more accurate to say that it
> is 'not the same as CRT' or something like that…..The ideas that
> we recognize that systems are not always fair because of race, and
> we value diversity, is a component of CRT. It's complicated and
> nuanced I admit, but that bullet in particular will be scrutinized
> by that opposing parent group.*

After reading this email, Ms. Ly accused Ms. Damikolas of trying
to *"soften"* the CRT language to deceive parents. (SIDENOTE: Ms.
Damikolas includes her pronouns in her email address block.) Returning

---

[33] Flavin, M. (2021) *Parents outraged after students in Orange County given 'white
savior complex' assignment: The gateway pundit: By Margaret Flavin, The
Gateway Pundit.* Available at: https://www.thegatewaypundit.com/2021/06/
parents-outraged-students-orange-county-given-white-savior-complex-assignment/

to the *Let's Roll America* news story on YouTube, Ms. Ly, while speaking before the Tustin school board, said oppressed versus oppressor lessons, classic CRT and Marxist themes, were being taught in Tustin's schools despite denials from school officials. She admonished TUSD for sneaking CRT tenets into Tustin classrooms. Ms. Ly then called their efforts to pass off CRT as something other than Marxist and racist as "despicable."

A third email, this one from high school Principal Michelle England, said she had been patient with parents, but was getting fed up. Her email read, *"I have a few very energetic parents right now over the issue of ethnic studies…I have been very accommodating up to this point, but am about to draw some boundaries."* In their reporting of the story, the *Gateway Pundit* said, *"Boundaries for what? To prevent parents from even asking questions about what information is being presented to their children?"*[34]

Another Tustin parent, Jon Schrank, also spoke at what appeared to be the same meeting attended by Ms. Ly. Documented in a second *Let's Roll America* video, this one on Rumble, Mr. Schrank said, *"Tonight, I find myself standing here for the sixth time in the last 12 months. Why do I keep coming back? Simple. I don't trust you."*[35] Mr. Schrank's main concern was a CRT version of math called *Equity Math.*

To further explain *Equity Math*, a new California Mathematics Framework (CMF) went into effect in July 2022. Much like CRT does with Ethnic Studies, CMF incorporates social justice issues into math lessons. Chapter 10 of CMF's official guidance defines mathematics as a highly racialized subject. Here's an excerpt from the CMF:

---

[34] Flavin, M. (2021) *Parents outraged after students in Orange County given 'white savior complex' assignment: The gateway pundit: By Margaret Flavin, The Gateway Pundit.* Available at: https://www.thegatewaypundit.com/2021/06/parents-outraged-students-orange-county-given-white-savior-complex-assignment/

[35] *CA parent demands transparency from School Board, Rumble.* Available at: https://rumble.com/vili35-tustin-school-board-one-parents-testimony.html

Inequities caused by systemic issues means that a "culture of exclu-sion" persists even in equity-oriented teaching. Many of the stories used to define mathematics, and to talk about who does or is good at mathematics, are highly racialized and English language-centric, and are experienced that way by students.[36]

If you had a hard time following that paragraph, don't feel bad. The grammar is horrible and the jumbled ideas are worse. As one reads the CMF curriculum, educators make Equity Math sound like a wonderful thing (they always do). In Chapter One, Equity Math is described as instruction that "elicits wondering" from students. Chapter Two further explains Equity Math moves away from rote formula memorization and sterile repetition which leads to disinterest in math. The CMF says connecting math to projects such as planting a garden leads to a higher level of understanding. Sounds like a wonderful idea, if simply applied in that manner.

Then, the CMF begins using phrases such as *culturally responsive teaching, sociopolitical consciousness,* and *historically marginalized people* (by now, the word "marginalized" should be familiar to you). It further describes how math should be used to counter racialized or gendered ideas. The CMF offers vignettes or sample lessons to teach math in ways supporting social justice. The following vignette uses math to address the subject of transgenderism to eleven-year-old children:

Ms. Ross teaches fifth grade at the Jackie Robinson Academy. She has been focusing on developing her students' sociopolitical consciousness through language arts and wants to bring mathematics into their thinking. To begin the process, the class is led in an analysis of word problems from their fifth-grade mathematics

---

[36] *Mathematics framework, Mathematics Framework–Mathematics (CA Dept of Education).* Available at: https://www.cde.ca.gov/ci/ma/cf/

*textbook. Ms. Ross selects three word problems to connect with
the class's current read-aloud of George, a novel by Alex Gino that
shares the story of a 10-year-old transgender fourth grader and
her struggles with acceptance among friends and family (CMF,
Chapter Two, p.64).*

We'll revisit the transgender children's book, *George*, more in Chapter
Four about North Carolina's Education Task Force, but, according to par-
ents like Mr. Schrank, when the transgenderism lesson begins, the math
lesson ends. Unsurprisingly, many Science, Technology, Engineering, and
Mathematics (STEM) professors and related professionals agree with Mr.
Schrank and do not approve of Equity Math.

In response to CMF adoption, STEM professors penned a letter to
California Governor Gavin Newsom, which said CMF *"politicizes"* K-12
math. By incorporating *social justice* and *racial equity* into math lessons, the
professors claimed California schools would *"de-mathematize math"* and
"build a mathless Brave New World on a foundation of unsound ideology."
Essentially, the professors believe CMF reduces time learning math and
uses that time to teach *social justice* instead. As of March 2022, 1,242 sig-
natories had signed the letter.[37]

Returning to Mr. Schrank, he and other parents worked for many
months to get answers from Tustin officials on numerous topics including
CRT. However, their questions often went unanswered. At one point,
TUSD Superintendent Franklin agreed to a Zoom call with parents. You
may remember, Mr. Franklin approved the *White Savior Complex* assignment and then told parents it wasn't authorized at TUSD.

---

[37] Evers, W. and Wurman, Z. (2021) *Replace the proposed new California Math Curriculum
Framework: Open Letter to governor Gavin Newsom, State superintendent Tony Thurmond,
the State Board of Education, and the Instructional Quality Commission: Williamson M.
Evers, The Independent Institute.* Available at: https://www.independent.org/news/article.
asp?id=13658

In my interview with Mr. Schrank in December 2022, he recounted his Zoom call with Mr. Franklin. Mr. Schrank said when the call started, Mr. Franklin didn't show up and two other school officials attended instead. The parents reminded the school officials they scheduled a meeting with Mr. Franklin, not with them. The school officials said Mr. Franklin was unable to attend, even though the Zoom meeting was on his public calendar.

Frustrated but not defeated, the parents began asking their prepared questions, but the school officials were unable to answer most of them. The parents asked them who had the answers, and the school officials admitted Mr. Franklin had them. From the parents' perspective, Mr. Franklin sent his assistants to run interference and the meeting was a gigantic waste of time.[38]

A second example of frustrating communications involved School Board member Allyson Damikolas, who wanted to soften the CRT language in Tustin's Ethnic Studies program. During the pandemic, TUSD held Zoom parent-teacher meetings instead of in-person gatherings. When parents asked Ms. Damikolas a difficult question, instead of answering, she often began talking about her scholarly credentials instead. For example:

> **Parent:** Please explain the CRT elements in this class curriculum.
>
> **Ms. Damikolas:** I have a chemical engineering degree from California State Polytechnic University at Pomona......

At one point, parents tried to recall Ms. Damikolas and two other TUSD school officials, but the attempt ultimately failed. During the recall, Ms. Damikolas participated in a Zoom meeting with an organization called *Women In Leadership* (WIL) that advocates for reproductive

---

[38] Interview with Jon Schrank, December 12, 2022.

rights. That means they're proabortion. During that Zoom meeting, Ms. Damikolas described her recall as an unsubstantiated effort by racist, White supremacist parents.[39]

Also, after the unsuccessful recall, the Los Angeles Times wrote a glowing story about Ms. Damikolas, which described parents' efforts as a *"campaign of lies and smears."* The Times story made sure to say TUSD does not teach CRT (there's that mandatory CRT denial again), but it does teach ethnic studies…which Ms. Damikolas supports.[40] You may recognize another pattern here. First, deny CRT, second, frame opponents as racists. In extreme situations, use like-minded friends in the press to help repair the reputations of public officials.

We return again to Mr. Schrank for a third example of communication problems between parents and Tustin school officials. In the same Rumble video previously mentioned, Mr. Schrank told the Tustin school board he sent two emails to each board member over his concerns with Equity Math. Only one out of nine responded. In the one email Mr. Schrank received, three questions were answered and four were ignored. Mr. Schrank noted answering three out of seven questions on any school test results in a failing grade. However, Mr. Schrank did learn one thing from this email exchange. The reply included a list of twenty-nine names on the TUSD Ethnic Studies Task Force. The group included sixteen TUSD employees, four parents, and nine members without an identified affiliation. Mr. Schrank defined this as a *"fraudulent, stacking the deck tactic."* For example, the sixteen TUSD employees could pass or stop any proposal by voting as a block, effectively overruling any input by the thirteen other members.

During Mr. Schrank's time before the School Board, he also recalled a Zoom meeting where he actually managed to speak directly to TUSD

---

[39] Interview with Jon Schrank, December 12, 2022.

[40] *Latina School Board Trustee in Tustin puts failed recall bid behind her* (2022) Los Angeles Times. Available at: https://www.latimes.com/socal/daily-pilot/entertainment/story/2022-02-24/latina-school-board-trustee-in-tustin-puts-failed-recall-bid-behind-her

Superintendent Franklin. During the call, Mr. Schrank asked questions Superintendent Franklin did not like. Instead of answering them, Superintendent Franklin got frustrated and abruptly hung up, ending the Zoom meeting. In Mr. Schrank's closing comments to the School Board, he told the Tustin school officials he would continue to challenge them for answers, and he would continue to make it known that TUSD officials have a *"commonality of deception and fraud."*

Now you may notice Ms. Ly and Mr. Schrank said *very* unflattering things to the Tustin School Board. They both basically called them liars to their faces. If you watch the video of Ms. Ly, she was nervous and shaking as she spoke. She definitely struggled to keep her emotions under control, but she heavily focused on a prewritten script and never lost her temper. Mr. Schrank also read from a prepared statement but was much calmer. Both presented facts which could not be disputed. For example, *"I sent out emails to nine school board members and only one answered."*

PRIMARY LESSONS: Ms. Ly and Mr. Schrank both presented very damning information to the Tustin School Board. They didn't pull any punches, but they also stuck to the facts and read from a script. They called the school officials *"liars"* without directly calling them names. *You have a commonality of deception and fraud.*

When speaking to your school board, stick to the facts and don't be afraid to tell the cold, hard truth. If you're unhappy, say so, but don't call anyone names or lose your temper. You don't want to give them any reason to kick you out of the meeting or define you later as a racist or terrorist in public comments.

Above all, it's a good idea to prepare and read from a script. Practice it several times before attending the meeting. If possible, read it in front of others. This has several benefits. First, it will tell you how much time you need to deliver your script. If parents are allowed two minutes to speak and your speech is three minutes long, you know you have to cut it down. This will ensure you get a chance to express all your thoughts during your given time. Next, it will help you keep your emotions in check. If you're nervous, stay focused on the written words. Eye contact with the school board is good, but not mandatory. Third, speaking the written word aloud helps you organize your thoughts more clearly. Do your comments make sense? Do they present complete ideas? Finally, if you get a chance to deliver your speech before a few volunteers, they can give you feedback and help you make improvements.

WHAT IS CRITICAL RACE THEORY?

Introduction

WHILE CRT SUPPORTERS try to decide if CRT is just a figment of everyone's imagination or real and should be defended, it's important for you to understand one thing. You *can* teach students of color about their ethnic history without shaming White students. Ethnic studies and CRT are **not** one and the same. Ethnic Studies programs do not require CRT, and anyone who says differently is lying to you. They lie a lot, don't they?

America is one of the most racially tolerant nations on earth. Surprised, aren't you? If you're dumb enough to watch the news these days, you often see *America-is-the-most-racist-nation-in-the-world* stories, one after another. Repeat a lie enough and it becomes truth. One problem. It's just not true. America is not the racist nation they unceasingly try to portray. Think about your relationships with your neighbors, friends, and co-workers of different races. Most of you probably get along just fine. If you don't, chances are the conflict is more about their actions and words, or yours, rather than the color of their skin.

Leftists consider the Europe Union (EU) to be the Holy Grail of racial tolerance. However, according to the *National Review*, unmanipulated research says America shines when compared to the EU regarding race relations.[41] I'm about to throw a lot of numbers at you. Sorry for that, but among National Review's findings from the *World Values Survey*:

- In France, 23% of people do not want a neighbor of a different race.
- In Sweden, only 36% of people believe diversity helps their country.
- In Greece, 63% of people believe diversity makes their country worse.
- In Spain, 31% of people believe diversity helps their country.
- In Italy, 53% of people believe diversity makes their country worse.
- Meanwhile, in America, 60% of people believe diversity makes the country better and only 7% say diversity makes it worse.

Also, without providing any numbers, the *National Review* names "India, China, the Islamic world, and the banlieue ghettos of France" as the gold standard for racism in the world. The article continues by saying the EU conducted a study on race relations after the George Floyd protests in America. Their commission was 100% White.

Furthermore, about 10% of EU citizens are ethnic minorities. According to the U.S. Census, the last time the U.S. was 90% White was in 1950.[42] At the same time, the *National Review* found, among all EU government employees, 99% are White and only 3% of European Parliament members are minorities. They also found the most diverse international institution in the European capital of Brussels is NATO — and for that you can thank the United States representatives who work there.

The *National Review* also says:

---

[41] Harsanyi, D. (2021) *America is the most tolerant place on Earth*, National Review. Available at: https://www.nationalreview.com/2021/10/america-is-the-most-tolerant-place-on-earth/

[42] *1950 census of population: Volume 4. special reports*, Census.gov. Available at: https://www.census.gov/library/publications/1953/dec/population-vol-04.html

By any genuine measurement, America is the most tolerant place on earth. This is an easy fact to forget for those who experience it. And these days, it's also an unfashionable thing to say. But the level of peaceful cooperation between people of truly diverse backgrounds, faiths, and creeds — or anything even approaching it — is wholly unprecedented in human history.[43]

In our racially tolerant culture, it's the CRT supporters who introduce racism into American society. One example is Robin Steenman's daughter. For a quick review, not once had Ms. Steenman's daughter ever described her playmates as a "Black girl" or a "White boy" until she watched a CRT-based video at school. She always described them, regardless of race, by the color of their shirt or the type of sneakers they wore. She was colorblind, but now, after watching the video, she describes her friends by race first.[44] They stole a piece of her childhood, and they plan to steal your child's innocence as well. In response, Ms. Steenman started a group called *Moms For Liberty*. We'll visit more with Ms. Steenman in Chapter 5, but right now, let's answer the question, *What is Critical Race Theory?*

Critical Race Theory Defined

In a *Newsweek* op-ed, the *Claremont Institute Center for the American Way of Life* produced one of the best CRT definitions I've seen so far. According to the Institute, CRT teaches children to hate themselves, their peers, and their country. When CRT supporters are asked to define CRT, they're often likely to deflect. In June 2021, *Slate* magazine published an interview

---

[43] Harsanyi, D. (2021) *America is the most tolerant place on Earth*, National Review. Available at: https://www.nationalreview.com/2021/10/america-is-the-most-tolerant-place-on-earth/

[44] *Kids are being propagandized with racism under critical race theory-interview with Robin Steenman* (2021) EpochTV. Available at: https://www.theepochtimes.com/kids-are-being-propagandized-with-racism-under-critical-race-theory-interview-with-robin-steenman_3895000.html

with Ibram X. Kendi titled, *Do critics of critical race theory even understand it?* [45]

Before we explore the understanding of CRT by its critics, I should introduce you to Dr. Kendi. He authored a book called *How to Be an Antiracist* calling for the creation of a new federal agency named the Department of Anti-Racism (DOA). Dr. Kendi's vision for the DOA:

> *...comprised of formally trained experts on racism and no political appointees. The DOA would be responsible for preclearing all local, state and federal public policies to ensure they won't yield racial inequity, monitor those policies, investigate private racist policies when racial inequity surfaces, and monitor public officials for expressions of racist ideas. The DOA would be empowered with disciplinary tools to wield over and against policymakers and public officials who do not voluntarily change their racist policy and ideas.*

Can you imagine the unchecked power of such an organization? Fortunately, for our nation, the DOA is DOA...dead on arrival. Getting back to the *Slate* article with Dr. Kendi, it begins with the sentence, "*Across the country, Republicans like Florida Gov. Ron DeSantis are fighting against critical race theory, even if they don't know what it is.*" This is one of the primary claims made by CRT supporters. Critics only fight CRT because they don't understand it. If critics only understood CRT, parents across the nation would openly accept it. They say these things at the same time they claim CRT doesn't exist and isn't taught in our schools.

I experienced this myself during a recent remote training session. To begin the training, the instructor asked each participant to introduce

---

[45] Johnson, J. (2021) *Do critics of critical race theory even understand it?, Slate Magazine*. Available at: https://slate.com/news-and-politics/2021/06/critical-race-theory-ibram-kendi-racism-racists.html?via=rss_socialflow_twitter

themselves. During my self-introduction, I mentioned I had returned to school to earn my Doctor of Education degree and was currently writing my Capstone project (a form of dissertation). He asked about the subject, and I told him Critical Race Theory.

He immediately said, *"What exactly is Critical Race Theory anyway? Besides it's not taught in schools."* He obviously had been very well educated in the standard protocols of CRT denial, but he didn't know with whom he was dealing. I calmly explained CRT was a Marxist ideology designed to divide people with racist principles. I added many school officials deny CRT, but their curriculums and internal communications say otherwise. The instructor didn't respond. You can imagine my surprise (not) when he later said his wife was an "ABC journalist."

Returning to Dr. Kendi, just one month after his interview appeared in *Slate* magazine, he wrote a CRT opinion piece for *The Atlantic*. If we piece together Dr. Kendi's public CRT statements from that time, we find conflicting information. This happens a lot with CRT as you probably have already noticed.

Here's the timeline. In June in *Slate* magazine, Dr. Kendi claims conservatives oppose CRT because they don't understand it. Just one month later in *The Atlantic*, Dr. Kendi called CRT a *fictional monster* designed to scare the American people. He also called efforts to portray CRT as a negative thing, the same as keeping African American children out of all-White schools in the 50s and 60s.[46]

To sum up Dr. Kendi's position(s), people only oppose CRT because they don't understand it. CRT is a fictional monster which doesn't exist. Even if CRT did exist, efforts to frame it as negative are racist. When you go back and forth on a subject like Dr. Kendi does with CRT, it can sometimes be tough to keep your story straight.

---

[46] Kendi, I.X. (2022) *There is no debate over critical race theory*, The Atlantic. Available at: https://www.theatlantic.com/ideas/archive/2021/07/opponents-critical-race-theory-are-arguing-themselves/619391/

Now let's take a moment to try to understand CRT from the opposing viewpoint. CRT supporters define CRT as both a theory and a set of tools that propose racism forms the core of our society. As a theory, CRT says Marxist class struggles divide societies into two basic groups, the poor or the oppressed and the rich or the oppressors. Just add racism to the mix and you have CRT. White people (and sometimes Asians) are the oppressors and people of color are the oppressed.

As a set of tools, CRT examines racism in any given social exchange with methods for gathering and analyzing data. Of course, if you look hard enough, you can find racism in anything, even between people of the same race.

Critical Race Theory Principles

In order for you to fully understand CRT, you must explore the tenets or principles of CRT. Scholars generally present five to seven principles when discussing the subject. During my research, I compiled eight CRT tenets. The following list contains each tenet with a brief description. Afterwards, we'll more thoroughly explore four of the more dominant CRT principles. The CRT tenets are:

1. *Systemic Racism.* Definition: Every major organization in our society oppresses people of color. Racism is a permanent fixture in American society and that will never change. The system marginalizes people of color and promotes White interests.

2. *Racism as Normal.* Definition: Racism exists everywhere in America. However, racism no longer primarily endures in extremist groups like the Klu Klux Klan. Instead, most racism occurs in lighter shades of gray in the everyday lives of average Americans.

3. *Interest Convergence.* Definition: White people only promote the interests of people of color when those interests also align with their own self interests. According to this tenet, President Abraham Lincoln freed the slaves, but only because it benefitted him and other White people.

4. *Race as a Social Construct.* Definition: There's no such thing as race and it has no basis in biology. No group has inborn characteristics different from or advantageous over other groups. White society invented race to oppress and exploit people of color.

5. *Differential Racialization.* Definition: Society treats different races of people in different ways. People of color are relegated to society's fringes, while White people continually occupy our culture's privileged positions. Our society marginalizes people of color in all possible ways.

6. *Intersectionality.* Definition: Social categories such as race, class, sexual preference, and gender are interconnected with overlapping influences. For example, a poor White man faces discrimination in only one category–class. Meanwhile, a poor African American woman faces discrimination in three categories–race, sex, and class. Furthermore, these disadvantages are not added together. They are multiplied. 1+1+1 does not equal 3. Intersectionality says it equals 6 or even 9.

7. *Counter-narratives.* Definition: These are stories told from the point-of-view of a marginalized person instead of the White version. It's accepted practice for counter-stories to be fictionalized to better capture the true racial essence of an experience.

Counter-stories may be completely true, partially true, or not true at all, but they always demand respect and consideration.

8. ***Whiteness as Property.*** Definition: The Smithsonian Institute defines *Whiteness* as White society norms and privileges by which all other races are compared.[47] An example might be many White people speak English with subtle regional accents. While people of color tend to speak English with stronger regional accents. When we apply *Whiteness* to this situation, people of color are often assumed to be less educated. Another example of *Whiteness*, the U.S. legal system is based on property rights. Since White people have allegedly always had the best access to valuable possessions, Whiteness is an asset and a privilege just like land or money.

Now let's further unpack the four most dominant CRT principles.

Permanence of Racism

The *permanence of racism* is the single most important CRT tenet. According to CRT supporters, racism became a fixture in our society when White people first stole indigenous lands after arriving in the Americas. Of course, relationships between indigenous peoples and colonial settlers weren't quite as black and white as CRT advocates want you to believe.

For example, King Charles II ceded Pennsylvania to William Penn in 1681 to pay off debts owed to the Penn family. However, the Lenni Lenape Indians still claimed ownership of this land. According to a letter obtained by the Historical Society of Pennsylvania, Mr. Penn then purchased that

---

[47] *Whiteness* (2022) *National Museum of African American History and Culture.* Available at: https://nmaahc.si.edu/learn/talking-about-race/topics/whiteness

same land from the Lenni Lenape to treat them fairly and ensure future peaceful relations.[48]

According to the *Clarke Historical Library at Central Michigan University* (CMU), this would later become the official position of the United States government in 1790. Our new nation determined purchasing land from indigenous peoples was far cheaper and less destructive than seizing it through war. From the CMU website:

> *When the first Congress of the new United States assembled in Philadelphia, it had exclusive power to set Indian policy. Article 1, Section 8 of the new Constitution stated, "Congress shall have Power . . . To regulate Commerce...with the Indian Tribes." Secretary of War John Knox, Secretary of the Treasury Alexander Hamilton, and President Washington all agreed Indian land was owned by the Indians and that the policy of the new government should be to purchase land from Tribal Governments. Few were surprised when Congress, in 1790, passed a law proclaiming that "no sale of lands made by any Indians, or any nation of tribe of Indians" would be valid unless "made and duly executed at some public treaty, held under the authority of the United States."[49]*

Essentially, in order for a land purchase to be legal, the Tribal Government and U.S. government must mutually agree to all features of the sale. Unfortunately, the *Clarke Historical Library* goes on to say one can find many examples of fraud in these purchases over the years, from both sides. Examples include Indians selling property without proper ownership

---

[48] *Letter from William Penn to the kings of the Indians in Pennsylvania, Historical Society of Pennsylvania.* Available at: https://hsp.org/sites/default/files/attachments/letter_from_william_penn_transcription.pdf

[49] *Land Transfers: Clarke Historical Library,* www.cmich.edu. Available at: https://www.cmich.edu/research/clarke-historical-library/explore-collection/explore-online/native-american-material/native-american-treaty-rights/land-transfers

and settlers assuming control of land tracks larger than represented in the sale. In order to fight this fraud, the U.S. government assumed control of these land sales and that policy remained in place for many years.

In fact, the Department of the Interior oversaw the sale of indigenous property as late as the 20th century. For example, the *California Indian Education* organization displays a poster on their website, dated from 1911, offering easy payments, perfect title, and possession of Indian land within 30 days.[50]

Unfortunately, one can find many examples in history which violated Constitutional intent behind indigenous land acquisitions. However, the main point is this, among the first real estate laws in the United States (in the Constitution no less), we find laws to protect the interests of both indigenous peoples and colonial settlers. This calls into question a number of CRT claims. First, did White people really steal the country from people of color as many believe? Second, were all U.S. laws written to protect the interests of and to consolidate power for White people only? It doesn't seem so.

Counter-narratives

Counter-narratives, or counter-storytelling, serve as another dominant CRT tenet. Counter-narratives are stories told from the point-of-view of people of color. They often differ greatly from the "White" versions. CRT supporters say counter-storytelling stops the silencing of minority voices. I think we can all agree hearing different perspectives of any story certainly has value. However, counter-narratives also come with elements which muddy the water.

For example, it's acceptable for CRT counter-stories to include real dialogues with fictionalized additions or even conversations which never

---

[50] *Indian land for sale* (1911) *Indian Lands For Sale US Department of the Interior 1911 Historical Poster.* Available at: https://www.californiaindianeducation.org/indian_land/for_sale/

occurred at all. Yes, it's perfectly acceptable for counter-narratives to exaggerate the truth. CRT proponents claim these adapted stories offer insights that may, otherwise, never come to light. From a cynical perspective, counter-narratives can add racist elements to a non-racial conflict to create the illusion of racism. However, no matter how much fictionalized content is added, counter-narratives must always be respected.

To explore further, let's use the example of academic achievement. Defined as the *achievement gap*, Asian and White students generally perform better academically than African American, Hispanic, and Native American students. CRT supporters tie this to race; however, some academic research ties this disparity more with class. For example, poor students from all races perform at lower levels than students of all races from families with higher incomes. Theoretically, families with less resources are unable to hire tutors when students fail. Higher income families can hire help to correct problems.

CRT proponents say the *achievement gap* proves systemic racism exists in our education system. Furthermore, they say denying race as the root cause of the *achievement gap* is an element of "Whiteness." CRT supporters believe racist policies and curricula purposefully produce lower academic achievement among students of color. In order to believe this, one must accept school officials across the country brainstorm strategies to confuse students of color. At the same time, those very same rules and lesson plans must inspire White and Asian children to succeed.

To further explain, let's tell the story of "Michele," a counter-narrative favored by one noted CRT scholar. The story says Michele is an underachiever due to systemic racism. The story begins with Michele repeatedly feeling marginalized by her school experiences. Michele majored in education and planned to become a teacher. For her schoolwork, she created lesson plans in ways that felt normal to her. When her White teachers marked them up, she believed they were trying to eliminate her blackness.

When Michele wrote an autobiographical essay for an assignment, her professor knocked off points for things such as grammar mistakes. Michele felt marginalized and thought, *how could anyone miss the point of her life in that way? How could anyone judge her personal experiences?* Michele felt marginalized again when counselors diagnosed her with a learning disability.

Despite the whiteness and other obstacles placed before her, Michele finally graduated. She landed a job as a teacher in a predominantly African American school. The school year began well for Michele, but soon her principal pressured her to teach in ways which did not feel natural to her blackness. Despite working in a school populated mostly by people of color, Michele felt disrespected because she was an African American woman.

As a counter-narrative, it's hard to know how much of Michele's story is true. For example, did Michele receive lower grades for her work because she was African American or did she receive lower grades because she needed to improve? Did her White professors mold her teaching methods to purposefully remove her blackness or were they trying to show her more effective teaching methods?

Michele even felt discriminated against when working with other people of color. Was it possible Michele had unrealistic expectations of the world around her? Was she unable to consider her shortcomings? Michele seemed to believe she had it all figured out. Perhaps Michele had much to learn about teaching and the color of her skin was not a factor. Of course, with counter-narratives, we never really know the line between truth and fiction.

Interest Convergence

Interest convergence says White society only promotes African American interests when those interests primarily support White interests first. For example, CRT supporters believe the government just wanted to pacify African American people when they honored Doctor Martin Luther King with a federal holiday. The government publicly claimed they created the holiday to honor a great African American man, but, through the lens of *interest convergence*, the real goal was to minimize disturbance to White society.

Affirmative action programs also face scrutiny under *interest convergence*. If we look up the definition of affirmative action, we find it helps people of color get equal access to positions and places of privilege. Those places of privilege include such things as promotions to management and acceptance to prestigious colleges. However, *interest convergence* says affirmative action programs were only designed for White interests and not to assist people of color. For example, according to *interest convergence*, White universities lowered admission standards for minorities so they could keep their systemically racist policies in place. It's a bit of circular logic. Colleges wanted to remain racist, so they allowed more people of color to attend so they could continue their racist ways.

CRT pioneer Richard Delgado believed affirmative action allowed a limited number of people of color to achieve, but not too many. Once they met the approved quota, the oppressors denied opportunities to the remaining students of color. In other words, affirmative action set an achievement cap to address the achievement gap.

For Delgado, the job of role model became undesirable. As a successful Hispanic college professor, he should inspire others; however, Delgado felt dishonest telling inner city students of color they could have a bright future. In fact, he called it "a very big lie: a whopper" in his 1991 scholarly article, *Affirmative Action as a Majoritarian Device: Or, Do You Really Want to Be a Role Model?*[51] Delgado claimed his law school enrolled about 35 Hispanic students per year for 16 years in a row. Delgado believed this showed stagnation in the advancement of students of color. He added that encouraging young people through affirmative action was bad for his soul.

---

[51] Delgado, R. (2005) *Affirmative Action as a Majoritarian Device: Or, Do You Really Want to Be a Role Model?*, Social Science Research Network. Available at: https://papers.ssrn.com/sol3/papers.cfm?abstract_id=2101428.

Derrick Bell, another CRT pioneer, used a counter-narrative from author Ellis Cose and his book, *The Rage of a Privileged Class*, to explain the CRT tenet of *interest convergence*. In the counter-story, when an African American professor arrived at a White university, his White colleagues were very friendly and supportive at first. Afterall, he was the very first African American professor at this particular school. Something good Leftists should celebrate, and they did.

However, Cose defined this behavior as patronizing. The White professors weren't accepting the new African American professor as an equal, they were really just congratulating themselves for their affirmative action policies. When the African American professor began to show he was a high achiever by getting published in important journals and being appointed to desired commissions, his White colleagues began to treat him with less enthusiasm. Through the lens of CRT, when the African American professor took things that "rightfully" belonged to the White professors, their moral support ended.

Intersectionality

Kimberle Crenshaw, another recognized CRT pioneer, made a name for herself when she first identified the CRT tenet of *intersectionality*. *Intersectionality* says various layers of discrimination build upon one another and create exponential forms of damage for victims. For example, African American women suffer from two forms of discrimination during their entire lives, racism and sexism. As they get older, they also suffer from ageism. If they're poor, they suffer from classism as well.

While studying Los Angeles battered women's shelters, Crenshaw found women of color often dealt with issues beyond the trauma related to battering and rape more often than White women. According to Crenshaw, women of color were also often burdened with poverty, childcare difficulties, and a lack of job skills. White women were as well, but in fewer numbers. These additional liabilities on program resources meant shelters, which predominately assisted women of color, helped fewer victims than shelters which mainly aided White women. 1+1+1 does not equal three. It equals six or nine or even twelve. As a CRT cynic, I'm not ready to completely embrace Ms. Crenshaw's theories, but I must admit the principle of *intersectionality* contains some truth.

Microaggressions

While not a direct CRT tenet, *microaggressions* are an important tool for CRT supporters. Remember, CRT is both a theory with principles and a methodology with tools to recognize racism. *Microaggressions* are defined as subtle snubs and insults directed at people of color.

Keep in mind, overt racism is illegal today. 75 years ago, you could openly say you didn't hire someone because they were Black. Today, that's a fantastic way to get sued, or worse. According to CRT proponents, most racism today occurs in the grey areas. That's where *microaggressions* come in.

On a side note, unfortunately, despite anti-racism laws, overt and socially acceptable racism does thrive in America today. But from my observations, the worst offenders are Leftists of *all races*, not conservative White people as you are told every day on the news. In fact, Leftists claim they see racism in everything. At this point, I believe they've convinced themselves this is true. However, the real reason behind their racism agenda, whether they know it or not, it's a particularly nasty and effective political tool.

One glaring example of a recent overt racist event occurred in the Boston Mayor's office. In December 2023, DailyMail.com published a story titled, *Boston's Woke Democrat Mayor Michelle Wu Plans Secret No Whites Christmas Party: Aide Accidentally Sent Group Email Invite Meant Only For 'Electeds of Color.'*[52] According to the story, a member of Mayor

---

[52] Potter, W. (2023) *Boston mayor Michelle Wu plans no Whites Holiday Party for councilors: Aide accidentally sent group email invite meant only for 'Electeds of color'*, Daily Mail Online. Available at: https://www.dailymail.co.uk/news/article-12859903/Boston-Democrat-Mayor-Michelle-Wu-christmas-party.html

Wu's staff sent party invitations to Boston's City Council members, which included seven White people and six people of color. The invitation read:

> On behalf of Mayor Michelle Wu, I cordially invite you and a guest to the Electeds of Color Holiday Party on Wednesday, December 13th at 5:30pm at the Parkman House, 33 Beacon Street.

A few minutes later, the staff member, Denise DosSantos, recanted the invitation for the seven White Councilors. DosSantos happens to be African American and includes her pronouns in her email signature block. Always a warning sign. Mayor Wu faced some criticism for her segregated holiday party, but I don't expect she'll lose her job over it. If she held a Whites-only Christmas party, she would've been impeached immediately and rightly so. She should've been impeached for her racist "Electeds of Color Holiday Party." No form of racism should have any place in our tolerant American society.

Returning to our discussion on microaggressions, in a courageous move (no, I'm not being sarcastic), academic researcher Dr. Scott Lilienfeld describes *microaggressions* as strong claims with inadequate evidence to support those claims.[53] And a 2014 opinion piece in the *Huffington Post* unwittingly seems to support Dr. Lilienfeld.

The article, written by Harvard professor Dr. John Fitzgerald Gates (three names, from Harvard, always a warning sign), both introduces *micro-aggressions* to popular culture and makes strong claims with inadequate evidence. In the article, Dr. John Fitzgerald Gates claimed *microaggressions* were the latest form of office racism. He added *microaggressions* taint inter-personal interactions all day long in modern American workplaces. In turn, this undermines workers' self-worth and productivity.[54]

---

[53] Lilienfeld, S. O. (2017). Microaggressions. *Perspectives on Psychological Science, 12(1),* 138-169. Available at: https://doi.org/10.1177/1745691616659391

[54] Gates, J. F. (2014). Microaggression: The new workplace bigotry. *HuffPost.* Available at: https://www.huffpost.com/entry/microaggression-the-new-w_b_5544663

Dr. John Fitzgerald Gates provided a few different examples to support his strong claims. One involved (then) Los Angeles Clippers owner, Donald Sterling. *TMZ*, the celebrity news organization, obtained a recording of Mr. Sterling telling his girlfriend, V. Stiviano, to not bring African American people to Clipper games. In the recording, Mr. Sterling was also unhappy Ms. Stiviano posted photos of herself associating with African American people on her social media accounts.[55] Oddly enough, Ms. Stiviano is both African American and Mexican.

Mr. Sterling later "apologized" during a CNN interview, but during his "apology," he called African Americans "the Blacks," he spoke of "owning" his players, and he strongly chastised Laker guard, Magic Johnson, for playing while HIV positive. Mr. Sterling, rightfully, faced severe consequences for his racist words. Eventually, the NBA banned Mr. Sterling for life and removed him as owner of the Clippers.

Returning to the *Huffington Post* op-ed, Dr. John Fitzgerald Gates connected Mr. Sterling's outrageous comments to an assumed culture of *microaggressions* in the Clippers' organization. Dr. John Fitzgerald Gates also said *microaggressions* cause $450 to $550 billion losses annually in U.S. workplaces. You don't have to be a genius to guess a racist like Mr. Sterling probably created a toxic culture within the Clippers' organization.

However, tying half trillion dollar loses to *microaggressions* is more difficult. Dr. John Fitzgerald Gates attributed these numbers to Gallup research but offered no link to the cited studies. To be fair, it's very likely poor interpersonal relationships do actually result in hundreds of billions of dollars in losses to American companies. But is racial conflict the first reason behind these unhealthy relationships as Dr. John Fitzgerald Gates claims? If he could prove it, I strongly suspect he would've provided

---

55 *Clippers owner Donald Sterling to GF — don't bring black people to my games ... including Magic Johnson* (2019) TMZ. Available at: https://www.tmz.com/2014/04/26/donald-sterling-clippers-owner-black-people-racist-audio-magic-johnson/

hyperlinks to the cited research. As Dr. Lilienfeld said, strong claims with inadequate evidence.

That reminds me of an old joke. It starts with *"Only an educated academic is stupid enough to believe…."* and ends with anything stupid that may be believed by your average academic. It's a pretty long list, but in this case, the joke goes, "Only an educated academic is stupid enough to believe in Critical Race Theory and *microaggressions."*

Using examples like Mr. Sterling, CRT supporters believe Americans are just as racist today as they were 75 years ago, they just hide it better. They don't consider the possibility that Americans have become more racially tolerant as the years pass. To explain how CRT supporters use *microaggressions* as a tool to expose today's more subtle forms of racism, researcher Dr. Angel Jones offered four questions to consider:[56]

1. *Did the aggressor intend to be racist?*
2. *What are the positives and negatives of responding to the microaggression?*
3. *Are there other witnesses who look like me and will support me if I make this stand?*
4. *Do I have the energy to deal with this?*

If one determines an interaction to be racist after using these questions, Dr. Jones recommends three basic responses which are refrain, reclaim, and reframe. Refrain means one fails to address a racist experience. Reclaim means one challenges racist behavior. Reframe involves engaging in an internal dialogue to better understand and perhaps appease the racism in a given experience.

To further explain the three recommended responses, Dr. Jones presents the counter-narrative of a young African American woman named

---

[56] Jones, A. M. (2021). *Conflicted: How African American women negotiate their responses to racial microaggressions at a historically white institution.* Race Ethnicity and Education, 1-16. https://doi.org/10.1080/13613324.2021.1924136

Tyesha, who sought academic advice from her White male professor. In the story, when Tyesha entered the professor's office, he confused her with a different African American female in the class. Tyesha did not look like the other African American female student and wondered how the professor could've mixed the two up. However, her inner dialogue considered they both wear braids.

She then wondered if the professor would confuse two White female students who wear both ponytails? Tyesha decided probably not and identified that moment as a *microaggression*. Unfortunately, she then let it derail the entire meeting. She allowed the conversation to drift into polite, yet unimportant topics and failed to ask for the specific academic advice she was seeking.

As a counter-narrative, all, some, or none of Tyesha's story may be true. However, the counter-story and Dr. Jones's questions reveal much. Imagine the negative emotional toll of constant focus on racism. Every single interaction at work or at school is potentially a *microaggression*. You walk past someone in the hallway. Maybe they say, "Good morning." Maybe they don't. Was this an intentional racist slight? What are the positives and negatives of addressing this? Are there others around who will support you if you do address it? Do you have the energy to do this? Now imagine repeating this routine dozens of times per day. How miserable would you be?

One problem with *microaggressions* is that they're defined exclusively by victim perceptions. If someone says something without racial intent, but someone nearby interprets it as racist, then that comment counts as a *microaggression*. No further discussion required. However, Dr. Lilienfeld, our rather brave anti-CRT researcher, contends a *microaggression* must have intent and must be obvious to others in the immediate area.

A second problem with *microaggressions*, they come with contradictory definitions. If a White person walks into a room occupied by several people and only one is a person of color, each individual greeting is a potential *microaggression*. If you greet the person of color first, others may see it as pandering. Someone else in the room may interpret that very same exchange as an example of a White person who is aware of their privilege. You can apply these rules in a million different ways.

Finally, CRT researchers often fail to consider personal conflicts and personalities. Maybe two people didn't exchange greetings because they just don't like each other and their races had nothing to do with it.

Critical Race Theory and Marxism

The foundation of CRT in Marxism goes back to *The Frankfurt School* during the early part of the 20th century. Marxist academics set up *The Institute for Social Research*, or *The Frankfurt School*, in Germany to explore ways to improve society. They're credited with creating *Critical Theory*, a philosophy which states the upper class uses capitalism and cultural institutions, like schools, to maintain power over the masses.

Add racism to the mix...tada!...you have *Critical Race Theory*. Therefore, according to CRT scholars, all institutions exist to reinforce White privilege and White supremacy over people of color. More recent Marxist thought on CRT ties it together with terms such as *Black radicalism, social justice,* and *anti-racism*. If you haven't noticed yet, *anti-racists* say some of the most racist stuff you'll ever hear. Remember, *anti-racists* aren't racist, just like anti-fascists aren't fascist.

Now there are minor, but key differences between each of these terms. For example, *Black radicalists* believe all Black people should unite as a single force, without regard to national citizenship, to end White supremacy around the world. They envision one Black super-nation without borders.

The next term, *social justice*, is defined by the United Nations (U.N.) as the "fair and compassionate distribution of the fruits of economic growth."[57] They always make it sound so nice, don't they? However, in a world ruled by

---

[57] *Social Justice in an open world* (2006) *United Nations*. Available at: https://www.un.org/esa/socdev/documents/ifsd/SocialJustice.pdf

social justice, I envision blue-helmeted storm-troopers ensuring the "equal distribution" of all wealth. If you don't cooperate, you can probably expect a good crack across the skull. It goes without saying, as god-like masters of society, our U.N. rulers would give themselves a much larger-than-normal share of goods. How do I know? Because that's how Marxists do everything.

The final term, *anti-racism,* is probably best explained by returning to Ibram X. Kendi's book, *How to Be an Anti-Racist.* Dr. Kendi says an *anti-racist* actively works against racism. He also says passively observing racism makes you a racist. From Dr. Kendi's book:

> One either allows racial inequities to persevere, as a racist, or confronts racial inequities, as an anti-racist. There is no in-between safe space of 'not racist.'

This is my second reference to Dr. Kendi, who sometimes separates himself from CRT. He defines himself as an *anti-racist,* one who actively works against racism, but he doesn't define himself as a Critical Race Theorist. In fact, during a debate on the subject with anti-CRT researcher Christopher Rufo, *The Federalist* reported Dr. Kendi denied being a Critical Race Theorist.[58] However, with all things CRT-related, we find conflicting information. Six months later, Dr. Kendi appeared on a *Slate* magazine podcast titled, *A Word…With Jason Johnson,* where he called CRT an inspiration and foundational to his work.[59] Here's where one might ask, if CRT is foundational to Dr. Kendi's *anti-racist* work, does that make him a Critical Race Theorist at some level? One might think so.

---

[58] Boyd, J. (2021) *Ibram X. Kendi falsely claims he is not a critical race theorist, The Federalist.* Available at: https://thefederalist.com/2021/06/24/ibram-x-kendi-falsely-claims-he-is-not-a-critical-race-theorist/

[59] Johnson, J. (2021) *Transcript—is critical race theory getting canceled?, Slate Magazine.* Available at: https://slate.com/transcripts/ekpZWlM0Z0hkVnQyaXlPVllGelBkWVNvRXk3cExkV0JYM2s5Zmw3bWVyZz0=

Another surprising contradiction found among CRT supporters, they believe *Whiteness* doesn't necessarily require white skin. Remember, the CRT tenet, *Whiteness as Property*, says *Whiteness* is both an asset and a privilege. However, some CRT proponents also claim *Whiteness* has fluidity. An African American can have *Whiteness* over another African American. One Latino can hold *Whiteness* over another Latino. Even a White person can have *Whiteness* over another White person.

Think back to Michele's counter-narrative. Michele was the aspiring teacher diagnosed with a learning disability, who felt her African American administrators were trying to take away her Blackness by asking her to teach in ways that didn't feel natural. Michele's counter-story also included recollections from her childhood which I didn't include when we visited her earlier. From her childhood memories, Michele recalled visiting her cousin when she was a girl. Michele is dark-skinned and her cousin is light-skinned.

As a dark-skinned African American girl playing dolls, her lighter skinned cousin always demanded Michele use the darker skinned doll because it looked like her. Under the *Theory of Fluidity*, Michele's cousin used the privilege of *Whiteness* to oppress her. Or maybe Michele's cousin was just an ill-mannered little girl. Keep in mind, as a counter-narrative, all, some, or none of Michele's story may be true.

PRIMARY LESSON: Critical Race Theory is a complicated subject. It isn't necessary for you to remember every single CRT tenet or related theory. The two CRT principles most commonly found are the *permanence of racism* and *differential racialization*. The *permanence of racism* refers to systemic racism. Under that CRT tenet, our entire society, including your child's homework, is designed to keep down people of color and cater to White people. *Differential racialization* refers to different treatment of different races. In particular, look for words such as *marginalization* and/or the *oppression* of one group over another.

As good Marxists, CRT scholars always pit one group against another (oppressed vs. oppressor). When researching for CRT in your school's curriculum, look for assignments that divide students by race and then create conflict. And above all, look out for *social justice* warrior training. Any assignment that requires studying the tactics of groups like *Black Lives Matter*, and then applies those tactics to new social issues is flat-out CRT. Don't let anyone tell you otherwise.

CRT Training

What does CRT training look like? We'll cover that in-depth over the next few chapters; however, I wanted to share one example with you before we get too deep into subjects like *California's Ethnic Studies Model Curriculum* in Chapter Three and *Wit & Wisdom* in Chapter Five. In 2021, the *Bongino Report* posted a video on Rumble of the beginning of a CRT training session titled, *CRT Instructor Warns Students Not to Tell Anyone Else.*[60]

At the 00:25 mark in the video, the instructor, Ms. Shari Revels-Davis,[61] explains the lesson is about *social justice*. CRT and *social justice* are two very similar terms sometimes used interchangeably as you may have already noticed. Next, at the 00:48 mark, Ms. Revels-Davis laid out three rules for the training, based on a book from Jason Reynolds titled, *Long Way Down.*

The three rules from *Long Way Down* are no crying, no snitching, and revenge. When Ms. Revels-Davis further explained "no snitching," she said, *"What's said in this class…,"* then waited for a student to finish the phrase.

---

[60] Bongino Report (2022) *CRT instructor warns students not to tell anyone else, Rumble.* Available at: https://rumble.com/vjj5g3-crt-instructor-warns-students-not-to-tell-anyone-else.html

[61] Nightingale, H. (2022) *Critical race theory high school instructor warns students not to talk about the class to anyone else, The Post Millennial.* Available at: https://thepostmillennial.com/critical-race-theory-high-school-instructor-tells-students-not-to-talk-about-class-outside-of-class

One student complied by saying, *"Don't leave this class."* The instructor, nodded her head with a big smile and responded with, *"Exactly."*

Anytime a teacher asks for secrecy, that is a bad thing. If CRT is a reasonable and appropriate framework for teaching racism as claimed by the NEA during their 2021 national convention, why did Ms. Revels-Davis tell students they aren't allowed to share the lesson with others? Unfortunately, the video ended before Ms. Revels-Davis could further explain revenge. That would've been interesting.

PRIMARY LESSON: Tell your child to tell you immediately if any school official ever tells them to keep a secret.

CHAPTER THREE

CALIFORNIA ETHNIC STUDIES MODEL CURRICULUM

Introduction

DESPITE VARIOUS CRT denials by California state educators, I personally found 519 direct references to CRT-related tenets in the first 600 pages in *California's Ethnic Studies Model Curriculum* (CESMC). CESMC includes 33 sample lessons for suggested use during Ethnic Studies classes. The sample lessons contain 391 CRT references. Most fall under systemic racism, the CRT tenet *permanence of racism*, and marginalization, the CRT tenet *differential racialization*.

I counted those numbers while doing research for my Capstone project, a dissertation-light if you will, while pursuing my doctoral degree at Liberty University. I used strict guidelines to identify these mentions. For example, they had to directly include CRT codes words such as *oppression* and *marginalization*. Merely implying those concepts was not enough to count as a CRT reference. If I hadn't conducted my research in that manner, the CRT references could have easily been in the thousands, because CESMC includes lots of "implying." Remember, California state educators claim CESMC does not contain CRT. Let's first begin by explaining CESMC.[62]

Assembly Bill 101 (AB 101)

California Governor Gavin Newsom signed AB 101 into law on October 8, 2021. At the time, existing laws encouraged California school districts to implement Ethnic Studies programs for grades nine through twelve. AB 101 makes Ethnic Studies mandatory for high school graduation starting with the 2029-2030 school year. This mandate put Ethnic Studies on par with other graduation requirements, such as two science classes, two math classes, and three English courses. AB 101 set the stage for CESMC.

CESMC Content

CESMC's primary CRT themes revolve around systems of power and the marginalization of minority groups, classic Marxist oppressor vs. oppressed group dynamics. However, another interesting theme shows up throughout CESMC's sample lessons, social justice activist indoctrination and training. Three lessons state this premise right in the title. They are titled, *Social Movements and Student Civic Engagement, Youth-led Participatory Action Research (YPAR),* and *#BlackLivesMatter (BLM) and Social Change.* The BLM lesson title includes a hashtag telling students how to track BLM on their favorite social media platforms. As you will soon see, CESMC was seemingly designed to train the next generation of BLM and *social justice* activists.

To ensure plausible deniability, CESMC frames most things in very positive ways. The introduction says Ethnic Studies *"helps bring students and communities together."* It builds *"greater understanding and communication across ethnic differences."* It reveals *"underlying commonalities that can*

---

[62] *Ethnic studies model curriculum (2021) Ethnic Studies Model Curriculum–Curriculum Frameworks & Instructional Materials (CA Dept of Education).* Available at: https://www.cde.ca.gov/ci/cr/cf/esmc.asp

bind by bringing individuals and groups together." And it adds, regardless of race, "*ethnic studies is designed to benefit all students.*" And this would probably all be true if the Ethnic Studies in CESMC didn't include Critical Race Theory.

However, as I read through CESMC, I noticed non-stop negative stereotyping in otherwise encouraging lessons. These are indicators of CRT and it's *Psychology of Shame.* For example, *Sample Lesson 8: An Introduction to African American Innovators* seems like it should be a very positive class and it is, for the most part. The lesson overview says, "*Students will be introduced to and explore the contributions of African Americans in science, technology, engineering and mathematics (STEM), literature and journalism, education, government and business/entrepreneurship.*" Sounds very inspiring.

However, when we look at the class's three suggested Essential Questions (overall themes students will study and identify), two come with negative connotations. The Essential Questions are:

1. *What contributions have African Americans made to the United States, and how has society benefited from them?*
2. *Why are some of these contributions not widely known?*
3. *How can these contributions be given greater recognition in society today?*

Yes, the lesson explores great African American achievements, but CESMC ensures the lesson tells students African American inventors never got full recognition for their work. Yes, there is certainly plenty of truth here, but does the lesson also say inventors of all races faced similar fates. What's the strongest possible explanation for most examples? Was it racism or just good ole fashioned greed?

Perhaps the most infamous example of an inventor robbed of their intellectual achievements is Nicholas Tesla. Mr. Tesla holds more than 700 patents around the world including the Alternating Current Induction

Motor, recognized as one of the top 10 discoveries of all time. That's the AC in AC/DC power. Modern society would not exist without it.[63]

Thomas Edison was working on a competing technology called Direct Current, or DC, around the same time. The competition between AC and DC became known as the War of the Currents. In the end, AC offered more efficient methods for sending electricity across long distances and it became the dominant power source around the world.[64]

However, Mr. Edison was a greedy and vengeful man. He soon began a nasty campaign to destroy Mr. Tesla's reputation. It was very effective and Mr. Tesla ended up selling his technology to a businessman named George Westinghouse for pennies on the dollar. Mr. Westinghouse went on to form one of the most powerful corporations of the 20th century. Mr. Tesla died alone and penniless in a New York City hotel room.[65] Mr. Tesla also happened to be White.

Returning to CESMC's sample lesson on African American inventors and the class's Essential Questions, the implied answers are obvious. Let's look at *Question #2: Why are some of these contributions not more widely known?* The question implies the marginalization of the true inventors due to systemic racism. Was racism the primary motivation behind marginalizing these inventions or did the inventors face the same greed and jealousy experienced by Mr. Tesla? The CESMC seemingly directs students to blame racism as the root cause.

Despite the obvious CRT references in CESMC, the California School Boards Association (CSBA) denies the existence of CRT in California

---

[63] *A life electric: The tragic and amazing story of Nikola Tesla, The Weekly Dose.* Available at: https://theweeklydose.org/a-life-electric-the-tragic-and-amazing-story-of-nikola-tesla/

[64] Nix, E. (2015) *How Edison, Tesla and Westinghouse battled to Electrify America, History.com.* Available at: https://www.history.com/news/what-was-the-war-of-the-currents

[65] *How Thomas Alva Edison stole Nikola Tesla's inventions and left Tesla penniless* (2022) *Tfipost.com.* Available at: https://tfipost.com/2022/01/how-thomas-alva-edison-stole-nikola-teslas-inventions-and-left-tesla-penniless/

schools. In fact, they say CRT rarely exists in any K-12 school. From the CSBA webpage on CRT:

> *There is no evidence that CRT is widespread in K-12 education. Although there is no definitive resource documenting the prevalence of CRT in schools, the consensus is that CRT is not included in curriculum and is rarely taught in K-12 schools.*[66]

Perhaps I should send Chapter One of this book to the CSBA, which documents Riverside Unified School District's Ethnic Studies program contains plenty of CRT. You may remember out of 27 published learning objectives, overall fifteen contain CRT principles and four include the words "Critical Race Theory" in their titles. But why quibble over small details?

Another difficult issue to explain is that CESMC authors openly claim they based the model curriculum on CRT. Manuel Rustin, chairman of the CESMC Advisory Commission, was quoted in an *EdSource* article saying, "*Ethnic studies without Critical Race Theory is not ethnic studies.*"[67] The article also claims teaching Ethnic Studies without CRT was schooling through the lens of White supremacy. The article said:

> *The most complex disagreement is foundational: Should teaching about past and current racial inequities and injustices be done primarily through the lens of white supremacy, the deliberate oppression by whites in America to gain and maintain power?*

---

[66] Macklin, K. (2021) *FAQs: Critical race theory,* California School Boards Association Blog. Available at: http://blog.csba.org/faqs-critical-race-theory/

[67] Fensterwald, J. (2022) *A final vote, after many rewrites, for California's controversial ethnic studies curriculum,* EdSource. Available at: https://edsource.org/2021/a-final-vote-after-many-rewrites-for-californias-controversial-ethnic-studies-curriculum/651338

The current CESMC is the fourth version of the curriculum and considered watered-down by CRT supporters. The first three versions were rejected for a number of reasons, including overt CRT components, leading to more than 100,000 complaints. They were too extremist even for crazy California. Let that rattle around in your head for a while. After far-left California Governor Gavin Newsom vetoed version two, many original curriculum writers quit or wanted their names removed from the project. They also wrote a protest letter to Governor Newsom which read:

> We urge the CDE not to give in to the pressures and influences of white supremacist, right wing, conservatives…and multiculturalist, non-Ethnic Studies university academics and organizations now claiming 'Ethnic Studies' expertise. [68]

To further explain the mindset of CESMC's original authors, the curriculum's first version liberally (LOL, right?) used phrases such as *hxrstory* to replace the word *history* in the Chapter 1: Introduction.[69] One can only imagine the smug and approving looks these "scholars" gave each other while using *hxrstory* instead of *history* in their spoken interactions.

How exactly does one say *hxrstory* anyway? I looked it up. The website *howtopronounce.com* says you spell the first three letters and then say, "story." Like this…H-X-R-Story.[70] Just imagine the clumsy roundtable discussions

---

[68] *Remove Names from Ethnic Studies Model Curriculum, A Letter from California Department of Education Ethnic Studies Model Curriculum Advisory Committee Members of 2019.* Available at: https://edsource.org/2021/a-final-vote-after-many-rewrites-for-californias-controversial-ethnic-studies-curriculum/651338

[69] *History-Social Science Subject Matter Committee, Attachment 1: Chapter 1: Introduction* (2019) *Instructional Quality Commission Agenda–Instructional Quality Commission (CA Dept of Education).* Available at: https://www.cde.ca.gov/be/cc/cd/iqcmay2019agenda.asp

[70] *Hxrstory pronunciation, Pronunciation Dictionary.* Available at: https://www.howtopronounce.com/hxrstory

which included *hxrstory* instead of just saying *history*. I guess we can add this to the list of things only an academic is stupid enough to believe and do.

CESMC's first version can be found on the California State Board of Education webpage from their May 16, 2019 meeting. If you choose to read it for yourself, the hyperlink is provided below. The very first paragraph reads:

> As early as the 1970s, some California public high schools began offering Ethnic Studies, positing that courses in the field would provide an opportunity to engage the hxrstory, cultures, contributions, perspectives, and experiences of groups that have been overlooked, hxrstorically marginalized, and often subjected to invisibility within mainstream courses.

Of course, *hxrstorically marginalized* is a clumsy and confusing way to say *historically marginalized*. Then it gets really weird:

> Ethnic Studies is about people whose cultures, hxrstories, and social positionalities are forever changing and evolving. Thus, Ethnic Studies also examines borders, borderlands, mixtures, hybridities, nepantlas, double consciousness, and reconfigured articulations, even within and beyond the various names and categories associated with our identities.

For those not immersed in woke academic culture, let's explain some of these words and phrases. I had to look them up myself, so don't feel bad. *Social Positionalities* defines your identity regarding race, gender, sexuality, etc.[71] *Hybridities* means a person with a blended background of two diverse cultures or traditions such as someone who has an African American

---

[71] *Positionality meaning* (2021) *Dictionary.com.* Available at: https://www.dictionary.com/e/gender-sexuality/positionality/

mother and a Latino father.[72] *Nepantlas* is an Aztec word for being in the middle of something.[73] The woke community defines nepantlas as being in-between cultures, not fully belonging to either. An example might include a Mexican immigrant, who, after spending time in America, is no longer completely Mexican. At the same time, as a citizen from another culture, he/she will never completely belong to American culture. When I got to *double consciousness* and *reconfigured articulations*, I lost interest in looking things up and moved on to a more enjoyable task.

Two years and three versions later, even after they removed all the hxr-stories, CESMC remains problematic. First, as already discussed, CRT curriculums are relentlessly negative and taxing on the students. For example, CESMC version four's Preface reads:

> *Ethnic studies courses address institutionalized systems of advantage, and address the causes of racism and other forms of bigotry including, but not limited to, anti-Blackness, anti-Indigeneity, xenophobia, antisemitism, and Islamophobia within our culture and governmental policies.*

Imagine the student depression that will result from these lessons. Next, CESMC says:

> *The Ethnic Studies Model Curriculum helps build the capacity for every young Californian to develop a social consciousness and knowledge that will contribute to the public good and, as a result, strengthen democracy.*

---

[72] *Hybridity definition & meaning, Merriam-Webster.* Available at: https://www.merriam-webster.com/dictionary/hybridity

[73] *Nahuatl-English translation :: Nepantla :: Dictionary, translatenahuatl.com.* Available at: https://www.translatenahuatl.com/en/dictionary-nahuatl-english/nepantla

When Leftists say things like "strengthen democracy," they always mean the opposite. Remember, they see capitalism and freedom as the problem, not the solution. In a capitalistic free society, they cannot guarantee the "fair and equitable" distribution of society's resources. Nor can they easily steal more than their fair share. Never forget, at their core CRT supporters are Marxists and that drives every decision.

Mirroring CRT's long-term goal of conquering capitalism and freedom, CESMC trains children to become social justice warriors. Sample lessons study the tactics of groups like *Black Lives Matter* (BLM), determine what worked, and then instruct students to use those strategies to address current "injustices" in their own communities. In Chapter Six, we discuss *Black Lives Matter at School*. Yes, *Black Lives Matter* designed a program to infiltrate America's schools. One other thing to remember about Marxists, they always target the children.

With this in mind, let's ask a few questions. For example, which BLM strategies will CESMC encourage students to use? Will it be the looting, the assaulting, and/or the burning down of buildings? Will they teach students that police departments intentionally target people of color and need to be defunded?[74] Will they encourage children to participate in riots based on false propaganda and to use slogans like "hands up, don't shoot?" *"Hands up, don't shoot"* was the misleading slogan used by BLM activists following the justified Michael Brown police shooting in Ferguson, Missouri.

To further explain, if you think back to the Michael Brown shooting which kicked off the Ferguson riots, just about everything you saw or read in the press was wrong. I'm going to explain to you what really happened according to the final Department of Justice (DOJ) report released on March 4, 2015. Unfortunately, by the time this information came out, the Ferguson riots were ancient history. The press, which relentlessly reported

---

[74] Cotton, T. (2021) *The BLM effect, National Review.* Available at: https://www. nationalreview.com/2021/07/the-blm-effect/

the misinformation associated with the shooting and the resulting riots, were only slightly interested in the final facts of the case.

According to the final DOJ report, the events leading up to the police shooting of Michael Brown began when Mr. Brown stole several packs of cigarillos from a convenience store. He also assaulted the store worker who tried to stop him and then escaped on foot.

Police Dispatch announced a robbery in progress and described two suspects over the radio. While patrolling the streets in a police SUV, Officer Darren Wilson found Mr. Brown and his accomplice walking down the middle of the street. They matched the descriptions of the robbery suspects, so he parked his vehicle in front of them to block their path.

Mr. Brown then prevented Officer Wilson from getting out of his SUV by blocking the door with his body. Mr. Brown reached inside the vehicle to punch Officer Wilson, grabbed for his weapon, and the two fought for control of the gun before Officer Wilson shot Mr. Brown in the hand. Mr. Brown then ran away and Officer Wilson chased him. Mr. Brown ran approximately 180 feet, stopped, turned around, and then charged Officer Wilson. That's when Officer Wilson fired the fatal shots.

Police Dispatch recordings show Officer Wilson was aware of the robbery and had suspect descriptions before stopping Mr. Brown. Claims that Officer Wilson stopped Mr. Brown for simply walking down the center of the street were false. DNA evidence found inside the police SUV prove Mr. Brown reached inside the vehicle. Claims that the initial struggle began outside the vehicle were false.

Bloodstain evidence shows Mr. Brown stopped running and charged back toward Officer Wilson. Additionally, autopsy evidence proves Officer Wilson shot Mr. Brown six to eight times in the front. Eyewitness claims that Officer Wilson shot Mr. Brown in the back were false. Other witness claims that Mr. Brown's hands were up in surrender when Officer Wilson shot him, execution-style, were also false.

In the end, every single person who participated in the *"Hands Up, Don't Shoot"* narrative in the press, recanted their stories, and admitted they never actually witnessed the shooting.[75] Unfortunately, by that time, the damage had already been done.

After the DOJ report came out, the press dutifully and seemingly reluctantly reported the facts. But only in their usual backhanded manner. It took twelve full days for the *Washington Post* to admit *"Hands Up, Don't Shoot"* was completely untrue and their admission came with the usual back peddling. Their article read:

> ..."*hands up, don't shoot" became the mantra of a movement. But it was wrong, built on a lie. Yet this does not diminish the importance of the real issues unearthed in Ferguson by Brown's death. Nor does it discredit what has become the larger "Black Lives Matter."*[76]

To review the *Washington Post's* take. Yes, *"Hands Up, Don't Shoot"* was a lie, but everything that happened afterwards was still justified. The *Washington Post* is not alone in that belief. For example, at the time of writing this book, on BLM's website, Mr. Brown's story gets top billing as one of the primary inspirations behind the organization. BLM's website reads:

> *In 2014, Mike Brown was murdered by Ferguson police officer Darren Wilson. It was a guttural response to be with our people, our family — in support of the brave and courageous community of Ferguson and St. Louis as they were being brutalized by law*

---

[75] DOJ report on shooting of Michael Brown (2015) www.justice.gov. Available at: https://www.justice.gov/sites/default/files/opa/press-releases/attachments/2015/03/04/doj_report_on_shooting_of_michael_brown_1.pdf

[76] Capehart, J. (2015) 'Hands up, don't shoot' was built on a lie, The Washington Post. Available at: https://www.washingtonpost.com/blogs/post-partisan/wp/2015/03/16/lesson-learned-from-the-shooting-of-michael-brown/

enforcement, criticized by media, tear gassed, and pepper sprayed night after night...In 15 days, we developed a plan of action to head to the occupied territory to support our brothers and sisters.[77]

Could this be the very same plan of action included in CESMC to be studied by California's children? Let's explore a few CESMC Sample Lessons.

Sample CESMC Lessons (not in numerical order)

CESMC includes 33 sample lessons. Several study the *Third World Liberation Front* (TWLF), a student protest in 1968 at San Francisco State College which demanded the creation of ethnic studies programs at the school. At that time, students of color felt their history classes didn't include enough information about African American, Hispanic, and Asian cultures. This was probably very true.

Some scholars credit the TWLF as the inspiration behind many modern social change movements. TWLF protests soon spread to other campuses, including the University of California at Berkeley. This led to the successful creation of race-based curricula such as Black Studies programs.

As we go through the sample lessons, you'll see a repetitive focus on themes of oppression, marginalization, systemic racism, and social justice activist training. The lesson guides also encourage students to explore their own personal histories. In other words, you may be a victim of racism, but don't realize it yet. Don't worry. We'll show you how.

Also, as we go through the lessons, make note of the concentration on negative occurrences. Imagine yourself as a student listening to the non-stop, relentlessly toxic messages about America, capitalism, and freedom. What would you think about this nation afterwards? Consider the intended purposes of the curriculum designers.

---

[77] *Herstory–Black Lives Matter, Black Lives Matter.* Available at: https://blacklivesmatter.com/herstory/

Sample Lesson 09: #BlackLivesMatter (BLM) and Social Change

This lesson studies police brutality incidents where unarmed African Americans were killed. The lesson recommends students undergo a BLM social change exercise where they explore their possible response to an incident in their community and consider the resistance tactics they might employ, similar to those created in 15 days in Ferguson, for example. Key terms taught in the class include racial profiling, oppression, police brutality, social movements, anti-Blackness, and resistance.

Lesson objectives include studying the effectiveness of BLM tactics for responding to police brutality. The class also provides legal instruction behind stand-your-ground, stop and frisk, noise ordinance, police officers' bill of rights, cash bail systems, 3-Strikes laws, prison abolition, and the death penalty.

The lesson advises students to contact grassroots organizations involved with their assigned topics and create community plans for change.[78] The most amazing part? California educators pretend this is all very normal.

Sample Lesson 02: Social Movements and Student Civic Engagement

This lesson seeks to align students with the Ethnic Studies Movement and other present-day social movements. Lesson objectives include researching social movements and understanding their tactics (again with the tactics training). In particular, the lesson recommends an in-depth study on key TWLF strategies, then compares them with modern-day social movements.

---

[78] Concha, J. (2020) *CNN ridiculed for 'fiery but mostly peaceful' caption with video of burning building in Kenosha, The Hill.* Available at: https://thehill.com/homenews/media/513902-cnn-ridiculed-for-fiery-but-mostly-peaceful-caption-with-video-of-burning/

Sample Lesson 11: Salvadoran American Migration and Collective Resistance

This lesson asks students to apply the *Four I's of Oppression* (FIOO) to El Salvadoran immigration. Apparently, nothing positive has ever happened to an El Salvadoran immigrant in America and FIOO is the only thing worthy of study. FIOO consists of ideological, institutional, interpersonal, and internalized oppression. No need to define each form of oppression. I'm sure you clearly see the class's focus on the negative.

Sample Lesson 21: Korean American Experiences and Interethnic Relations

The lesson explains that Korean Americans were marginalized during the 1992 Los Angeles (L.A.) riots. The two most significant events from the riots include the beating of African American Rodney King by L.A. police and the shooting of African American Latasha Harlins by Korean liquor store owner, Soon Ja Du.

Both incidents occurred in March 1991. Du went to court for the shooting of Harlins and received a light sentence with no jail time. Not long afterward, the police officers involved in the Rodney King beating were given not guilty verdicts. The L.A. riots were the result. The sample lesson also says the L.A. riots inspired present-day social movements such as *Black Lives Matter* (BLM).

Sample Lesson 05: Introducing Dominant Narratives

Despite repeated claims that CESMC does not include CRT, *dominant narratives* share a direct connection to the CRT principle of *counter-narratives*. To refresh your memory, the dominant narrative of the Michael Brown shooting would be the "police version" of the events which say the shooting was justified. The counter-narrative would be the version presented on BLM's website which claims a White police officer murdered an unarmed African American young man without justification.

From a CRT perspective, dominant narratives force the creation of counter-narratives because the dominant stories silence marginalized voices. Remember, counter-stories may contain all, some, or none of the truth, but must always be respected.

The lesson tells students dominant narratives gain public acceptance through repetition. In other words, once dominant narratives become normalized, systems of power maintain them, and create the illusion of objectivity. The lesson suggests students reflect about the ways dominant narratives benefit oppressor groups and injure oppressed groups. The sample lesson also recommends students create journals to document dominant narratives they witness outside school.

Sample Lesson 03: Youth-led Participatory Action Research (YPAR)

YPAR engages students with social change movement resources and inspires them to become engaged participants. YPAR provides students with examples of social issues to study and then guides them to create solutions. No hiding it. Completely transparent Social Justice Warrior indoctrination boot camp.

The lesson recommends high school students develop presentations about their selected social issue and then share them with middle and elementary school students. In other words, once the high school students are brainwashed, they begin indoctrinating younger kids. Yes, they are absolutely coming for your children. The sample lesson states YPAR should specifically study people with marginalized histories and overlooked counter narratives.

Conclusion

As previously mentioned, when one explores the sample lessons, certain themes certainly emerge...*systems of power, marginalization* of oppressed groups, and *social justice* indoctrination. CESMC is also designed to be more than just an ethnic studies class. It's designed to be incorporated into the entire school culture and other educational subjects as well. From CESMC's *Chapter Two – District Implementation:*[79]

> *...administrators should work to weave the purpose, benefits, principles, and impact of ethnic studies into the fabric of the school, and as a means to partner with parents and the broader community...It is especially important to establish connections between the new program and existing offerings in history–social science and English/language arts. Additionally, ethnic studies can be integrated into existing courses in addition to, or instead of, creating a standalone ethnic studies course.*

According to this paragraph, CESMC plans to implement CRT principles, not only in the Ethnic Studies programs, but also in all classes and even in the entire community. In Chapter Two, CESMC recommends creating "steering committees" to indoctrinate administrators, teachers, students, parents, and other community members. Yes, they are coming for your children, but they are also coming for you.

PRIMARY LESSON: Take the time to read your child's course descriptions. It's important and they can usually be found online with a simple search. You never know what you'll find. Don't expect the find the words Critical Race Theory, but look for code words such as *...systems of power, systemic racism, oppression, marginalization,* and *social justice.*

---

[79] *Ethnic studies model curriculum (2021) Ethnic Studies Model Curriculum–Curriculum Frameworks & Instructional Materials (CA Dept of Education). Available at:* https://www.cde.ca.gov/ci/cr/cf/esmc.asp

CHAPTER FOUR

NORTH CAROLINA TASK FORCE

Introduction

LEFTISTS HAVE TAKEN over North Carolina's schools and they're indoctrinating your children. Those were the reports received from parents and teachers by Lieutenant Governor Mark Robinson even before he assumed office on January 9, 2021. He quickly established a task force to investigate. The complaints began with the implementation of the state's 2021 Social Studies Standards. For example, one lesson objective for American History states:

> *Explain how the experiences and achievements of minorities and marginalized peoples have contributed to American identity over time in terms of the struggle against bias, racism, oppression, and discrimination.*[80]

By now, you probably recognize the CRT code words *marginalized* and *oppression*. In response, the *Fairness and Accountability in the Classroom for Teachers and Students Task Force* (FACTS) created a website where

---

[80] *North Carolina Standards for American History* (2021) *Public Schools of North Carolina.* Available at: https://drive.google.com/file/d/10D3-Ka1eFqset4zp_LFM0WP-AgV9ohd6/view

parents and school officials could report any witnessed indoctrination. By the summer of 2021, FACTS published a report titled, *Indoctrination in North Carolina Public Education.*[81] At the time of publishing, the Task Force received more than 500 submissions and identified six main themes. The FACTS website remained open after the report was published and, almost two years later, received an additional 300 entries according to Lieutenant Governor Robinson's staff who I interviewed in February 2023. Two themes were directly related to CRT; however, all six were disturbing. Those themes are:

1. *Fear of Retaliation*
2. *The Sexualization of Kids*
3. *Critical Race Theory (CRT)*
4. *White Shaming*
5. *Biased News Media and/or Lesson Plans*
6. *Shaming of Certain Political Beliefs*

The FACTS website received reports of political indoctrination from every region of the state, particularly urban areas. Much like in California, FACTS submissions show CRT happens in many school subjects, not just ethnic studies classes. Also, like in California, some school districts published official pro-indoctrination policies showing CRT exists in the overall school culture.

For example, the Durham County Board of Education established the first week in February as the annual *Black Lives Matter at School (BLMAS) Week of Action.* Yes, there is such a thing as *Black Lives Matter at School.* The National Education Association (NEA), the nation's largest teachers'

---

[81] F.A.C.T.S. report (2021) F.A.C.T.S. Report | Lieutenant Governor Mark Robinson. Available at: https://ltgov.nc.gov/facts-report-summary/open

union, documents the participation of BLMAS in more than 200 schools.[82] Yes, they are coming for your children. More on BLMAS in Chapter Six.

Media Response

It goes without saying, the left-leaning press attacked FACTS, but they were particularly hateful against Lt. Gov. Robinson, who happens to be a conservative Republican...and an African American. They always attack African American conservatives with a special kind of venom. WRAL News in Raleigh even published a political cartoon depicting Lt. Gov. Robinson's efforts to improve education as the work of the Klu Klux Klan.[83]

The *Charlotte Observer* published a series of scathing editorials on the FACTS report even before its release. Using classic Saul Alinsky-inspired tactics (if you're doing something wrong, charge your opponent with doing the same), they accused Lt. Gov. Robinson of trying to indoctrinate children. An editorial titled, *Stop Harassing NC Teachers With Your Indoctrination Police Mark Robinson*, published on March 26, 2021, said:

> *Robinson, who is Black and an unlikely ambassador for white, conservative grievance, assumed the state's second highest political office in January. He has taken up the role of being ill-informed and divisive with gusto...the lieutenant governor thinks his top priority should be challenging the motives of teachers and fueling paranoia about schools indoctrinating children.*[84]

---

[82] *Black lives matter at school* (2024) National Education Association. Available at: https://www.nea.org/resource-library/black-lives-matter-school-week-action

[83] *Draughon draws: Learning social studies* (2021) WRAL.com. Available at: https://www.wral.com/draughon-draws-learning-social-studies/19504379/

[84] *Stop harassing NC teachers with your indoctrination police, Mark Robinson* (2021) Charlotte Observer. Available at: https://www.charlotteobserver.com/opinion/

On August 24, 2021, after the FACTS report came out, the *Charlotte Observer* published another editorial with another even-handed title (sarcasm intended). The op-ed was titled, *Lt. Gov. Mark Robinson's Truly Wacky Idea for North Carolina Public Schools*. The article used a slight-of-hand quote from Lt. Gov. Robinson to make him appear as if he wants to remove science from elementary schools. It's the type of under-handed tactic that Leftists often use. The quote in the story comes from Lt. Gov. Robinson's book titled, *We Are the Majority: The Life and Passions of a Patriot*. The editorial said:

> (from Lt. Gov. Robinson's book) *"In those grades, we don't need to be teaching social studies," he (Robinson) writes. "We don't need to be teaching science. We surely don't need to be talking about equity and social justice."*
>
> *Because learning about scary liberal concepts like plants or geography is clearly a threat to elementary school children. Does he think kids need to wait until middle school to learn that the earth isn't flat?*[85]

Sounds bad, doesn't it? Yes, Lt. Gov. Robinson said those things about social studies and science, but he said them in reference to the failure of NC schools to teach basic skills such as reading, writing, and math. The *Charlotte Observer* edited that paragraph to make Lt Gov Robinson seem out of touch. To show you Lt. Gov. Robinson's real intent behind his words, page 248 of his book says:

[85] *Lt. Gov. Mark Robinson's truly wacky idea for North Carolina public schools* (2022) Charlotte Observer. Available at: https://www.charlotteobserver.com/opinion/article264811369.html

The way to do this is to demand proficiency in reading, writing, and math in grades one through five. In those grades, we don't need to be teaching social studies. We don't need to be teaching science. We surely don't need to be talking about equity and social justice. I'll say it again: we need to be teaching kids how to read, how to write, and how to do mathematics.[86]

As you can clearly see, the sentences before and after that cherry-picked quote change everything. NC schools need to teach children basic skills before moving on to more advanced subjects. Sounds radical and wacky, right? Yes, sarcasm intended.

You can be sure of one thing. The *Charlotte Observer's* "journalists" intentionally attempted to deceive their readers. Even the national press took time to attack Lt. Gov. Robinson by calling him, "*…an eager participant in (the Republican) mission to keep America ignorant.*"[87] I personally believe Lt. Gov. Robinson should run for President someday. At the time of publishing this book, he was running for Governor of North Carolina and for the good of the state's public schools, I hope he wins.

Let's dig deeper into Lt. Gov. Robinson's demand for academic proficiency in his book. First, you need to know NC schools are a disaster. According to the *2019 Reading State Snapshot Report* from the *National Center for Education Statistics* (NCES), only 36% of NC fourth graders were proficient or better in reading.[88] THIRTY-SIX PERCENT!!! This is what Leftists defend.

---

[86] Robinson, M. (2022) *We are the majority!: The life and passions of a patriot.* New York, NY: Republic Book Publishers.

[87] Jones, J. (2022) *North Carolina's Mark Robinson reportedly floats ban on science, history in elementary schools,* MSNBC. Available at: https://www.msnbc.com/the-reidout/reidout-blog/mark-robinson-north-carolina-science-history-ban-rcna44386

[88] *2019 reading North Carolina Grade 4 snapshot report,* National Center for Education Statistics. Available at: https://nces.ed.gov/nationsreportcard/subject/publications/stt2019/pdf/2020014NC4.pdf

A Tweet from Brian LiVecchi, Lt. Gov. Robinson's Chief of Staff, further explains:

> For kids who aren't reading at grade level, promoting them to higher grades with more rigorous and complex subject matter that requires independent reading for success is not helping them. Those kids must be able to read before we throw biology at them, or we set them up to fail.[89]

After the FACTS report came out, the *Charlotte Observer* again attacked it with another charming opinion piece with another dandy title (sarcasm intended). The article was titled, *North Carolina's Indoctrination-in-Schools Witchhunt was a Big, Embarrassing Dud.* The op-ed, published in August 2021, said:

> Teachers will recognize what Robinson delivered Tuesday — a report with a lot of dressing and little meat. It's the term paper of a student who didn't do the work and didn't have much to offer. It was a dud.[90]

A report with more than 500 eyewitness submissions defined as a "dud." Really? Let's take a look.

---

[89] LiVecchi, B.P. (2022) *For kids who aren't reading at grade level, promoting them to higher grades with more rigorous and complex subject matter that requires independent reading for success is not helping them. those kids must be able to read before we throw biology at them, or we set them up to fail.*, Twitter. Available at: https://twitter.com/BLiVecchi/status/1561845690094993413

[90] *North Carolina's indoctrination-in-schools witchhunt was a big, embarrassing dud* (2021) *Charlotte Observer.* Available at: https://www.charlotteobserver.com/opinion/article253728098.html

FACTS Findings

Let's review the findings behind the "dud" FACTS report titled, *Indoctrination in North Carolina Public Education Report Summary*.[91] Before we get started, one interesting thing the report uncovered is that NC teachers use an educational resource website titled, *Learning for Justice Club*, which offers more than 6,000 CRT-related resources. State officials never authorized the website nor the materials it provides. I guess the big question here. Why is it being used?

Remember, the Task Force organized submissions into six categories, including The Sexualization of Kids. Since this book explores CRT in schools, I will largely skip this section for now. However, I intend to cover this subject with a future book, but there's one FACTS submission I want to include here to give you an idea of the age-inappropriate content being taught to your children in school. It's about a book called *George* by Alex Gino.

Please keep in mind a number of FACTS submissions contain grammatical and other errors. Presumably, the report left the errors intact to retain the authenticity of the submissions. The submission about *George* said:

> *George by Alex Gino is a children's book used in North Carolina classrooms (which) illustrates a biological boy in the fourth grade who wants to be a girl. The book talks about cutting off male genitalia and hormone therapy. The submitter who shared this information said the book was included in their child's elementary school. This book is recommended for third- to seventh-grade students. An excerpt from the book is below:*

---

91 *Summary of indoctrination in North Carolina Public Education Report* (2021) *Scribd*. Available at: https://www.scribd.com/document/521521007/ Summary-of-Indoctrination-in-North-Carolina-Public-Education-Report

"So, like, do you want to"—he made a gesture with two fingers like a pair of scissors—"go all the way?" George squeezed her legs together. "Maybe someday," she said.

The FACTS report says educators used books like *George* to share ideas about sex and gender with children with which parents may disapprove. In some cases, FACTS findings revealed school administrators instructed teachers to lie to parents about their child's sexual identities and preferences. Yes, they are coming for your children.

FACTS Submissions

The following submissions are presented here as published in the FACTS report. Again, they sometimes contain grammatical errors. They are reproduced here as submitted. Most examples feature excerpts from much longer submissions. Comments in parathesis (like this), are my remarks. Also, throughout this book, I italicized quotes from books and print articles. Due to the length of these submissions, for easier reading, I left them in normal font.

One more reminder before we begin, the following submissions fall into five categories which include *Fear of Retaliation, Critical Race Theory, White Shaming, Biased News Media and/or Lesson Plans*, and *Shaming of Certain Political Beliefs*. Other than the previous section on *George*, I left out submissions for the sixth category, *The Sexualization of Kids*. Here are the submissions:

> Our teacher of the year at school has a BLM decoration on her door at school with a big fist. Today, the same teacher posted on social media a picture of herself in a t shirt that says "Blue lives murder." However, I am not allowed to wear any political apparel supporting Republicans…Please do not post my identity. I'd lose my job.

My son is being put through a learning unit in his activism with videos on how to become an activist with discussion and topics of climate change, gun control, racial discrimination, and gender equality. My son was even asked in a survey about what activist issues are important to him, and felt pressured to respond with the answer of racial discrimination...he is afraid to speak out for fear of being penalized by his school and or teacher.

My daughter chose to stay on Mute the majority of the year. Those that agree with [the teacher's] point of view got positive attention. Those that did not, such as our daughter, who had the courage to join the conversation that day, were told in chat to "Back down", "Calm yourself", "Some are going to try to make it hard on the majority of us who want equality for all".

My daughters quickly learned to just write papers from the teacher's point of view to get an A, and that's exactly what they got. They wrote countless papers supporting the BLM movement, although they didn't support it as they are not racists nor were raised to be. But with so much focus on racism, they just played the game.

Not only are the teachers indoctrinated and teaching the same indoctrination, but the curriculum in all the classes is all about race and gender. Every single book/passage reading in AP English class is about white supremacy/privilege.

...all of the lessons for homeroom for Black History Month and women's history month have all included people who are

Democrats and NO conservatives. Why could we not celebrate the first Lieutenant- Governor who was an African American?

After speaking with my son after he became visibly upset, I learned that his teacher was promoting anti-religious, anti-law enforcement, sexual orientation and anti-American assignments...I contacted the teacher and met with her to determine if my son could be transferred to another class. After this meeting, a meeting was scheduled with the school's principal and again I asked for my son to be removed from this class. Again my request was denied....a meeting was finally set up with the Director of Secondary Education...When I asked about the assignments she was issuing as part of her class I was told that it was part of a state mandated "Social Injustice" curriculum and so I asked for a copy of that curriculum. I was told it could be found on the State Education Department website but no link existed. (author's comment: Yes, they're lying to you.)

This is the mission statement of Hairston Middle School in Greensboro...At Hairston Middle School our mission is to unify families and members of the community to destroy ALL barriers and systems of oppression by utilizing anti-racist teaching along with cultural responsiveness so that student voice is amplified through international mindedness as we prepare social justice agents of change. (author's comment: This mission statement remained on Hairston Middle School's website for more than a year after my initial investigation. It was finally removed in 2022. The grammatical errors alone are STUNNING. These are the people teaching your children to read and write. Also notice they are intentionally preparing social justice agents of change.)

On Monday, 01 February, the counselor for Tucker Creek Middle School in Havelock, NC sent an email to all school staff containing links to Black Lives Matter, Inc curriculum as part of "celebrate BLM week". In the email, the counselor ... explicitly encourages staff/teachers to utilize and implement the BLM, Inc curriculum resources in their classrooms. (author's note: More on *Black Lives Matter at School* in Chapter Six.)

The straw that broke the camel's back for us was when a white male teacher made his class of 20 students (including my daughter) play the 'privilege game'...All students line up horizontally and then the teacher calls out certain things and you take a step forward or backwards accordingly. For example, if you have ever been discriminated against because of your skin color, take a step back. If your parents are divorced, take a step back. By the end of the exercise, a white male was in front and a African American female was in the back with everyone else in between.

His teacher refers to the students as "my comrades" and "my little activists." I've heard her discuss the current political climate often. For example, in discussing the January 6 Capitol incident, she told the students, "Trump promoted violence." She's openly supportive of BLM

This same teacher also gave an assignment to do a mini-biography during Black History Month and decided to only include current liberal figures to report on. There was no option for Martin Luther King Jr or Mark Robinson [THE 1ST AFRICAN AMERICAN LIEUTENANT GOVERNOR

IN NC!!! How is that not a worthy name to include considering he is from GREENSBORO???] Only options for Barak
Obama, Kamala Harris, and several liberal athletes.

Entire class is social justice warrior (SJW) training. First
assignment was a reading from Marx and to explain how the
theories apply to today's society. Last quiz included a question
requiring him to identify all of his white privilege.

...each student was asked whether they supported BLM or
not. They had to respond and it was made very clear by previous comments by the teacher that to not support BLM was
to be on the wrong side...The teacher was also pro socialism
and pushed socialist ideology. For example he told the students that "the only reason your parents don't like socialism
is because all they think of are the bad parts of communism"

I apologize if the number of submissions overwhelmed you a bit.
However, the main point, the *Charlotte Observer* read the FACTS report
and these very same submissions, plus an addition 485 or so. Then declared
the report "*a big embarrassing dud.*" Nothing here to see. I reached out to
the *Charlotte Observer Editorial Board* to get a comment on the FACTS
report and their op-ed saying it was a big embarrassing dud. Of course, I
received no response.

FACTS Report Aftermath

In May 2021, North Carolina lawmakers used submissions from the
FACTS website to create House Bill 324 (HB 324) titled, *Ensuring dignity & nondiscrimination/schools.* HB 324 prohibits teaching the superiority of one race over another and that people are inherently racist based
on skin color. HB 324 also forbids making students feel guilty for society's

past sins and framing the United States as a fundamentally racist nation. Additionally, HB 324 bans forcing teachers and students to confirm their belief in CRT-related concepts.[92] Critics of HB 324 framed the bill as an attempt to eliminate authentic teaching and an attempt to advocate for White supremacy (of course).

In an editorial written for the news outlet, *Common Dreams*, Dr. Brian Gibbs says HB 324 uses fear to intimidate educators and encourages parents to threaten teachers directly. If you think back to the FACTS submissions, it seems the only teachers who feel intimidated are those who oppose CRT. Dr. Gibbs' article titled, *North Carolina's New Education Bill Promotes Historical Erasure and White Supremacy*, (another adorable title) also says HB 324 attacks efforts against racism and oppression. The article says:

> *What they are concerned with is control…the authors of HB 324 and the F.A.C.T.S. Task Force want to engage in acts of historical erasure, avoidance, and advocacy for white supremacy. The weapon the authors and supporters of these measures are using is fear. If the measures themselves don't cow and intimidate educators the hope is that the mob, that people will be so incensed that they begin to threaten educators themselves.*[93]

To learn more about *Common Dreams*, I took a look at their *About Us* webpage. There I found statements such as, "*We share our readers'*

---

[92] Gwyn, B. (2021) *HOUSE BILL 324: Ensuring dignity & nondiscrimination/schools.* Available at: https://dashboard.ncleg.gov/api/Services/BillDocument/2021/51556/1/H324-SM-NBC-8949

[93] Gibbs, B. (2022) *North Carolina's new education bill promotes historical erasure and white supremacy, Common Dreams.* Available at: https://www.commondreams.org/views/2022/02/08/north-carolinas-new-education-bill-promotes-historical-erasure-and-white-supremacy

progressive values of social justice, human rights, equality, and peace."[94] There's that phrase again...social justice. Also, Dr. Gibbs is an assistant professor from the College of Education at California State University at Los Angeles...of course.

HB 324 passed through NC's House and Senate. However, on September 10, 2021, North Carolina Governor Roy Cooper vetoed it. Gov. Cooper is obviously a Democrat who opposes Lt. Gov. Robinson's efforts to eliminate CRT and increase parental involvement in NC schools.

Deterred but not defeated, the NC Senate introduced Senate Bill 49 in January 2023. Senate Bill 49 was also known as the "Parents' Bill of Rights" (PBR...no, not Pabst Blue Ribbon). Gov. Cooper also vetoed the PBR. However, this time, Gov. Cooper's veto was overridden and the PBR became law in August 2023. The PBR recognizes a parent's primary role in raising their children and guarantees their right to direct their education, moral upbringing, and healthcare. Hard to believe North Carolina had to put that in writing. The PBR also requires state employees, such as school administrators, to notify parents immediately if their child experiences anything that may impact their physical, emotional, or mental health.[95] Again, hard to believe North Carolina had to put that in writing.

Perhaps the most important feature of the PBR is that the law requires timely feedback for parental concerns. The PBR demands all parental concerns to be resolved within 30 days. Not just addressed but **resolved** within 30 days. If not resolved in 30 days, parents may request a formal hearing with the State Board of Education. The PBR also requires the involved public school to pay the administrative costs of the hearings, and the court may force the school to pay the parents' attorney fees as well. No more ignoring parents' emails in North Carolina!

---

[94] *About Us* (2022) *Common Dreams.* Available at: https://www.commondreams.org/about-us

[95] *Senate Bill 49 / Parents' Bill of Rights, North Carolina General Assembly* (2023) ncleg. gov. Available at: https://www.ncleg.gov/BillLookup/2023/S49

Worried about being accountable to parents, the NC Board of Education wrote a letter of concern to North Carolina legislators.[96] From my reading, the letter was primarily concerned with the workload behind addressing parents' concerns.

The PBR also bans gender identity and sexuality instruction for kindergarten through fourth grade. No more family-friendly drag queen shows in the school library. Additionally, the PBR establishes penalties for any state employee who encourages children to keep secrets from their parents.

Critics say the PBR will hinder relationships between educators and students, as well as threaten the safety of gay and lesbian students.[97] Yes, I understand many parents struggle accepting a gay or lesbian child but placing a teacher in between them leaves too much opportunity for exploitation, in my opinion.

As of February 2024, *FutureEd*, a Left-leaning think tank funded by organizations such as the Bill & Melinda Gates Foundation, was tracking 85 similar "parental rights bills" and says they exist in 26 states.[98] One thing is crystal clear. Nationwide, parents are demanding greater access to their children's education, and that is a good thing.

PRIMARY LESSONS: When parents stand together, they can drive real change. Get in touch with like-minded parents, have meetings, create an agenda, and deliver it to school leaders…together.

---

[96] *Letter to the North Carolina General Assembly* (2023) *Public Schools of North Carolina, State Board of Education.* Available at: https://ednc.wpenginepowered.com/wp-content/uploads/2023/06/Letter-to-the-GA-SB-49-2023-V7.pdf.

[97] Vinueza-McClellan, H. (2023) *State Board discusses parents' bill of rights and graduation requirements in new budget, EducationNC.* Available at: https://www.ednc.org/state-board-discusses-parents-bill-of-rights-and-graduation-requirements-in-new-budget/

[98] DiMarco, B. (2023) *Legislative tracker: 2022 parent-rights bills in the States, FutureEd.* Available at: https://www.future-ed.org/legislative-tracker-parent-rights-bills-in-the-states/

Also, truly sympathetic leaders do exist. Your teacher has a boss, your principal has a boss, and your school board members have a boss. They may be hard to find, but keep working until you find an ally in the chain of command. Hopefully, you won't have to go all the way to your Lieutenant Governor's office.

Finally, as you proceed, keep the title of an Anne Coulter book in mind, *Never Trust a Liberal Over 3—Especially a Republican.* Pay attention to actions, not words. Be wary of school administrators and teachers who tell you nice things to make you happy, but then rarely deliver. And certainly do not let school officials get away with lying to you.

One more thing, start voting for people who respect parental rights!

CHAPTER FIVE

WIT & WISDOM IN TENNESSEE

Introduction

ROBIN STEENMAN'S DAUGHTER watched one 13-minute CRT video at school, and she suddenly became focused on race among her friends. In response, Ms. Steenman founded *Moms For Liberty* (MFL) to dig deeper into the subject. You may remember Ms. Steenman from Chapter Two's introduction.

To revisit Ms. Steenman's story, not once had her daughter ever described her playmates as a Black girl or a White boy until she watched a CRT-based video at school. She always described them, regardless of race, by the color of their shirt or the type of sneakers they wore. She was colorblind, but after watching the video, she described her friends by race first.[99] In 13 minutes, they stole a piece of her childhood.

Moms For Liberty

MFL soon identified a reading program in local Tennessee schools called *Wit & Wisdom* (W&W). In W&W, they found frequent racially-charged

---

[99] Philipp, J. (2021) *Kids are being propagandized with racism under critical race theory-interview with Robin Steenman, EpochTV.* Available at: https://www.theepochtimes.com/kids-are-being-propagandized-with-racism-under-critical-race-theory-interview-with-robin-steenman_3895000.html

topics, age-inappropriate subjects, and recurrent dark themes, such as negative stereotypes toward White people, anti-Americanism, anti-religion, suicide, and cannibalism.

W&W readings vigorously pointed out America's shortcomings, but never touched upon its redeeming qualities. Many illustrations lacked even one single smiling face. Ms. Steenman decided to discuss the impact of recurring negative stories on young children with a doctor. The doctor identified it as the *Psychology of Shame*.

During an interview with *The Epoch Times*, Ms. Steenman explained the impact on children when exposed to the *Psychology of Shame* and CRT.[100] The results, according to Ms. Steenman, children sometimes say they're ashamed to be White or get harassed because they're White. They're made to feel responsible for things like American slavery. Some children even begin to think about suicide. Others fantasize about murdering their family.

The *Psychology of Shame* can also happen to adults. When MFL reviewed W&W materials for their investigation, the daily readings often depressed the parents. If W&W can disheartened adults in this way, imagine the impact on children. While W&W never mentions CRT specifically, its lessons often include classic oppressor vs. oppressed themes. Something we've seen over and over. They remove the words "Critical Race Theory," but leave the content in the lesson materials.

To combat racially divisive education programs like W&W, the Tennessee House of Representatives passed House Bill 580 in May 2021. While the bill never mentions CRT, Amendment Number Two specifically bans any curriculum with ideas such as racial superiority, inherent

---

100   Philipp, J. (2021) *Kids are being propagandized with racism under critical race theory-interview with Robin Steenman*, EpochTV. Available at: https://www.theepochtimes. com/kids-are-being-propagandized-with-racism-under-critical-race-theory-interview- with-robin-steenman_3895000.html

racial privilege, the United States as incurably racist, and other similar concepts.[101] Despite the law's passage, many CRT opponents say CRT tenets remain in Tennessee's educational curricula, in programs like W&W.

In December 2021, MFL researched W&W in Williamson County schools' curricula and published their discoveries in a report titled, *Let's talk Wit & Wisdom: A presentation of parents' findings*.[102] Here are some of the age-inappropriate themes found in W&W readings:

Kindergarten – murder
1ˢᵗ Grade – graphic mating, gender fluidity
2ⁿᵈ Grade – anti-police, anti-fire department
3ʳᵈ Grade – anti-church, torture
4ᵗʰ Grade – rape, murder, adultery, scalping/skinning, stillbirth
5ᵗʰ Grade – gore, excessive violence, alcoholism, promiscuity, harmful
  relationships

Great Minds, the company behind W&W, says they build their programs on the belief all children are capable of greatness. They always make it sound so nice, don't they? One side item, *Great Minds* used to be called *Common Core*. In case you're not familiar, 40 states adopted *Common Core* in 2010 with remarkable bipartisanship. However, the program was a disaster and most schools cancelled it within four years.[103] From these "*Great Minds*," we now have W&W. The lesson here. Leftists rarely abandon their plans.

---

[101] *House Bill 580, Tennessee House of Representatives* (2021) *Tennessee General Assembly.* Available at: https://www.capitol.tn.gov/Bills/112/Amend/HA0441.pdf

[102] *Let's Talk Wit & Wisdom: A presentation of Parents' Findings* (2021) *Moms For Liberty, Williamson County Chapter.* Available at: https://momsforlibertywc.org/wp-content/uploads/2022/01/LTWW5-2-Dec-21.pdf

[103] McArdle, E. (2014) *What happened to the Common Core?, Harvard Graduate School of Education.* Available at: https://www.gse.harvard.edu/news/ed/14/09/what-happened-common-core

It goes without saying, the *Great Minds* website very clearly states they do not teach CRT.[104] However, when we explore MFL's findings in *Let's talk Wit & Wisdom*, we find CRT tenets throughout the lesson plans, age-inappropriate content, and the *Psychology of Shame*. Here are some suggested books in W&W readings:

Kindergarten:

Why Mosquitos Buzz in People's Ears by Verna Aardema. This book tells the story of a mother owl trying to feed her babies. While she was away from the nest getting food, a monkey killed one of her children. From the book:

> ...she was still out searching for one more tidbit to satisfy her hungry babies. When she returned to the nest, she found one of them dead. Her other children told her that the monkey had killed it (author's note: The illustration on the next page shows an angry monkey ready to smash an owlet in the head with a stick. Two other owlets watch in fear).

Rap A Tap Tap: Here's Bojangles – Think of That! by Leo & Diane Dillon. In this story, Bojangles is an African American man who loved to dance. In the story, many angry White people refuse to watch him. They always close their doors or turn away when they see Bojangles coming. The accompanying teacher's manual includes passages such as:

> Some doors were closed to Bojangles because of the color of his skin...Bojangles kept dancing even though some people wouldn't watch him....I see a man that is turned away from Bojangles. That door is closed...Share that Bojangles lived during a time when many doors were closed to him because of the color of his skin.

---

[104] *The facts about wit & wisdom®–and its impact*, Great Minds. Available at: https://greatminds.org/the-facts-about-wit-wisdom-and-its-impact

The teacher's manual repeatedly directs children to focus on the negative aspects of the story, such as extreme Jim Crow-style racism in places like the American South. Certainly, an important subject to teach, but how many kindergarteners possess the maturity to handle such a subject? Not many, if any at all, in my opinion.

The lesson includes the CRT tenets of *differential racialization* and *systemic racism*, without naming them, of course. In addition, the vast majority of the White faces in the illustrations are angry in an over-the-top manner when looking at Bojangles.

First Grade:

Sea Horse: The Shyest Fish in the Sea by Chris Butterworth. This story teaches the reproductive processes of sea horses. The female creates the eggs. The male carries them and gives birth to the offspring. From the book:

> Sea horses are the only male fish to get "pregnant" like this, growing their young inside their own bodies.

Then the accompanying video ties the sea horse reproductive process to gender identity and fluidity. From the video:

> We humans tend to think of who we are as mostly fixed. But in the ocean, identity can be a fluid and mysterious thing.

Actually, no. In the ocean, there may be examples of fluid gender identity, but seahorses are not one of them. Male and female seahorses don't switch gender roles. Females always create the eggs. Males always carry them until they hatch. No swapping of identities or genders involved. Another example of Leftist slight-of-hand "facts."

Brave Irene by William Steig. This book features a young girl carrying a box through a heavy snowstorm, obviously a difficult task. At one point,

Irene finds herself completely covered in snow and contemplates suicide. From the book:

> ...she plunged downward and was buried. She had fallen off a little cliff....Even if she could call for help, no one would hear her. Her body shook. Her teeth chattered. Why not freeze to death, she thought, and let all these troubles end. Why not? She was already buried.

In the end, Irene digs her way out of the snowbank, but why teach first graders about giving up and freezing to death? A very odd way for first graders to find their "greatness."

Feelings by Aliki. This book features several short stories with illustrations designed to help children explore their feelings. In one short story, a boy travels to a cave inhabited by a dragon. From the book:

> The smell of eaten children filled the boy's nostrils.

Do you want your first grader reading about the smell of eaten children? Also, the teacher's manual instructs teachers to tell students to explore their feelings during their reading. The two suggested feelings are furious or sad. Out of 32 feelings identified in the book, 22 were negative. The four feelings most mentioned were:

Mad/Angry – 154
Sad – 79
Happy – 41
Excited – 18

Consider the *Psychology of Shame* when reading those numbers.

Second Grade:

Martin Luther King Jr. and the March on Washington by Frances E. Ruffin. This book obviously tells the story of MLK. Certainly a worthy chapter in American history. However, MFL objects to the negative tone of the book. MLK certainly has a positive and age-appropriate story to tell, but the authors overlooked this side of his history. From the book:

> *At sit-ins, Black people take seats in "white only" restaurants or theaters. And they refuse to leave. Often they are dragged out. Sometimes they are put in jail...There are signs that say "For Whites Only." Even water fountains say "White" or "Colored."*

Photos in the book show angry White firefighters spraying a fire-hose on African American protestors and different water fountains for different races. Yes, all historically accurate, but are they appropriate for second grade?

The CRT principles included in the book are *systemic racism* and *differential racialization*, different treatment between races. One could also add *race as a social construct* (race was invented by White people to keep other races down) and *Whiteness as property* (White people have access to more valuable assets than people of color).

Ruby Bridges Goes to School: My True Story by Ruby Bridges. Another historically accurate, but overtly negative book perhaps better read by older and more mature children. From the book:

> *A long time ago, some people thought that Black people and white people should not be friends. In some places, Black people were not allowed to live in the same neighborhoods as white people.*

Illustrations in the book include a famous Norman Rockwell painting with a racial epithet clearly written on a wall in the background. The teacher's manual instructs teachers to point out the racial slur if the children miss it. If second-graders don't know the "N" word before reading this book, teachers will make sure they do after completing this lesson. Accompanying photos include White people holding up signs that read:

> We won't go to school with negroes

> We want white tenants in our white community

Yes, the book is historically accurate, but is it appropriate for second graders? CRT components include *differential racialization, systemic racism, racism as normal, race as a social construct,* and *whiteness as property.* But the words "Critical Race Theory" don't appear in the book, so that means it doesn't contain CRT, right?

One more book:

Separate is Never Equal: Sylvia Mendez & Her Family's Fight for Desegregation by Duncan Tonatiuh. This book might be the worst of them all. It contrasts the different school experiences of White and Hispanic children. From the book:

> *They have generally dirty hands, face, neck and ears....*

> *"How many children...at the Mexican school are inferior to whites in personal hygiene?" asked Mr. Marcus.*

> *"At least, seventy-five percent."*

> *"In what other aspects are they inferior?"*

> *"In their economic outlook, in their clothing, and in their ability to take part in the activities of the school."*

A cow pasture surrounded the school. The students had to eat their lunch outside, and flies would land on their food. There was an electric wire that surrounded the pasture to keep the cows in…the school did not have a playground – not even a swing.

The illustration for that last passage only shows Hispanic children eating lunch with flies buzzing around them. In the background, you see cows, a cow patty, and an electric fence. It reminds one of a gulag. Another illustration shows White children swimming in a pool and Latino children kept out by jail-like bars. A sign reads *"No Dogs or Mexicans Allowed – Public Pool."*

W&W's Implied Curriculum

MFL deeply explored a nine-week W&W module for second graders titled, *Civil Rights Heroes.* Sounds like a nice title, right? However, MFL found most lessons focus on injustice and oppressor vs. oppressed indoctrination. The teacher's manual mentions injustice 314 times. It requires students to create a nonverbal sign for injustice and signal every time they identify an injustice during the nine-week module.

If you remember, much of *California's Ethnic Studies Model Curriculum* centered on creating social justice activists. This W&W module does as well. On Day Five the module asks, *"What makes a good protest song?"* The lesson includes a sing-a-long to a song titled, *Ain't Gonna Let Nobody Turn Me Around.* From the lyrics:

> *Ain't gonna let Jim Crow turn me 'round*
> *Turn me 'round, turn me 'round*
> *Ain't gonna let Jim Crow turn me 'round*
> *I'm gonna keep on walkin' Keep on talkin'*
> *Marchin' to that freedom land*

Why exactly did they choose that song for a sing-a-long? It is because every city in America is trying to reinstitute Jim Crow laws? If you were a W&W student, you might think so. As the module progresses, the activism training gets more direct. The Day 32 lesson is titled, *"How can 'children' respond to injustice?"* On Day 33, the lesson is, *"How can responding to injustice impact the world?"* Then on Day 34, *"Why is it important to respond to injustices?"*

You'll notice each of these themes elicits a *social justice* response from 7-year-old children. In their review of W&W, MFL notes second graders lack the critical thinking skills and maturity to properly understand the positives and negatives of history, especially when W&W largely leaves out the positives in their lesson plans. From the report:

> For 9 weeks, Wit & Wisdom focuses repeatedly and daily on very dark and divisive slivers of U.S. history. The narrow and slanted obsession on historical mistakes reveals a heavily biased agenda, one that makes children hate their country, each other, or themselves.

Yes, this is the *Psychology of Shame* and you can imagine it's impact on 7-year-olds.

Wit & Wisdom Adoption

MFL reports W&W never passed Tennessee curriculum standards, yet somehow it was implemented. In fact, it failed multiple reviews. Then it appears typical Leftist slight-of-hand tactics were employed to install it anyway. Here's a rundown of how it happened.

According to MFL's report, in June 2019, the Tennessee State Board of Education (TSBOE) received their first W&W failing test results. Eleven days later, discouraged but not defeated, the TSBOE changed the scoring protocol to be more W&W friendly. Then, in August, the TSBOE fired all five current reviewers and hired two new ones. Two reviewers are easier to control than five, right? In September, a new review begins under the "watchful eye" of the TSBOE. In October, despite their best efforts to fix the game, W&W fails again. This time, the TSBOE tires with the unsophisticated peasants on the review board. They overrule the appraisal results and approve W&W.

In order to do this, the TSBOE used a trick called a *"materials already in use"* waiver. Apparently, many school districts were already using W&W during the review without prior approval. From MFL's report, *"Districts already using failed materials under a pilot program could continue doing so."*

The TSBOE granted 70 curriculum waivers, 33 for W&W. Then, to prop up W&W, the TSBOE begins publishing and providing its own free supplemental W&W materials for schools to use. Sounds like someone at the TSBOE was very determined to subject Tennessee's children to W&W and the *Psychology of Shame*.

PRIMARY LESSONS: Study the curriculum at your child's school. Most of the time, it can be found online. Again, you probably won't find the words "Critical Race Theory," but look for concepts such as *marginalization, White supremacy, oppression,* and *systemic racism*. If you find those code words, especially in subjects unrelated to Ethnic Studies, your child's school is indoctrinated in CRT.

CHAPTER SIX

BLACK LIVES MATTER AT SCHOOL

Introduction

BLACK LIVES MATTER (BLM), yes, the same Black Lives Matter that burned down cities across the nation a few summers ago, while Globalists/Leftists cheered them on and donated billions of dollars to their cause(s), also created something called *Black Lives Matter at School* (BLMAS). Yes, they are absolutely coming after your children.

Black Lives Matter at School

BLMAS provides BLM-approved educational materials for use in American classrooms. Unfortunately, BLMAS has a close working relationship with the *National Education Association* (NEA), the nation's largest teacher's union with affiliates in 14,000 schools. The NEA offers toolkits for use during BLMAS's *Week-of-Action*. BLMAS designates the first week of February as a *Week-of-Action* for social justice. As mentioned earlier in this book, the NEA's website diligently documents the participation of more than 200 schools in the BLMAS curriculum.[105]

In 2022, the BLMAS *Week-of-Action* encouraged protests against anti-CRT legislation in 27 states. Again, they say CRT isn't taught in our

---

[105] *Black lives matter at school* (2024) *National Education Association.* Available at: https://www.nea.org/resource-library/black-lives-matter-school-week-action

schools, but if CRT isn't taught, what are they defending? Why the need to organize nationwide protests against anti-CRT efforts?

In 2023, BLMAS designated the entire year as *A Year of Purpose* with five different national events planned during February. For example, BLMAS established Monday, February 06, as *Write Night with Free Minds Book Club*. Here's the description of the event:

> *Writing workshop exploring the poetry of incarcerated youth, as part of our commitment to attend to systems and networks of care to make the domination, erasure, and dehumanization of Black life obsolete.*[106]

Here we have another example of *Psychology of Shame*. Non-stop focus on the negative. Even with positive leaning events with wonderful sounding descriptions, there's always an underlying negative element. *Author's note:* The reference hyperlink below takes you to BLMAS's calendar on the current month you're reading this book. As of February 2024, you can still find the description of this event by navigating the calendar to February 2023.

One national event covered historically Black colleges and universities to discuss their histories and their benefits to African Americans. Sounds very positive, but BLMAS had to include the negative as well. They framed the evening as an unapologetic look at the history and creation of Black colleges. One can anticipate the non-stop focus on the worst stories they could find.

A second national event was called the *Black Joy Party Connection Space*. Sounds like a positive and fun event. Even the event description sounds nice:

> *A space to be your authentic self, celebrate, and be in community! To collectively love and care for one another as extended intergenerational families.*

---

[106] *Black Lives Matter at School Calendar*, BLM at School. Available at: https://www. blacklivesmatteratschool.com/calendar.html

Again, it sounds positive on the surface. However, if we take a moment to look deeper into these words, the description says the event provides a space for African Americans to be "authentic." The underlying message here, American society is a place where African American people are not free to be themselves. Notice the synergy in ideologies between CRT and BLMAS.

Black Lives Matter

Before we dig into BLMAS more, it's important to understand BLM. You may be someone whose primary exposure to BLM occurred during the riots. You may remember "journalists" on TV speaking glowingly about the group with looters and burning buildings behind them. Patrisse Cullors, Alicia Garza, and Opal Tometi founded BLM in 2013 following the acquittal of George Zimmerman for the self-defense killing of Trayvon Martin. Zimmerman founded a neighborhood watch program when his Florida gated community experienced a crime surge. He soon began patrolling his neighborhood.

One night during his rounds, Zimmerman noticed Martin walking down the street. Zimmerman called the police and identified Martin as "suspicious." At this point, Martin noticed Zimmerman and asked why he was following him. Zimmerman says Martin then attacked him, pinned him to the ground, and began beating him.

That's when Zimmerman shot Martin in self-defense. The evidence at the scene and two recorded phone calls support this version of events. Zimmerman and Martin were both on the phone before the attack. When police arrived, Zimmerman had a bleeding head wound and grass on the back of his shirt. A trial found Zimmerman properly acted within Florida's Stand your Ground law.[107]

---

[107] Donaghue, E. (2013) *George Zimmerman verdict: Trayvon Martin confronted neighborhood watch volunteer, defense attorney says, CBS News.* Available at: https://www.cbsnews.com/news/

Leftists rarely miss an opportunity to fund-raise when a tragedy occurs. After Zimmerman's not guilty verdict, BLM was born and their spin campaign began. BLM used Trayvon Martin's death as proof America was a nation where White supremacists hunted Black children in the streets, despite the fact Zimmerman is Hispanic. The press dutifully called Zimmerman a "White Hispanic" as they seemingly attended BLM strategy meetings and happily carried out their portion of the plan.[108] Remember, the worse they can make an event sound, the more money groups like BLM can raise. For "journalists," that means more viewers.

In a 2015 interview with *The Real News Network* (TRNN), BLM's Patrisse Cullors called Zimmerman, a *"light-skinned, White-passing man."* Again, Leftists tend to say the most racist things you've ever heard. That same interview also revealed the political background of BLM's founders. Ms. Cullors said:

> *Myself and Alicia (Garza) in particular are trained organizers. We are trained Marxists. We are super-versed on, sort of, ideological theories.*[109]

Breitbart reported on the 2015 TRNN interview in 2020 and further defined Ms. Cullors' and Ms. Garza's ideologies as radical Marxist-Leninist.[110] Britanica.com defines the ideologies of Marxism-Leninism as:

---

george-zimmerman-verdict-trayvon-martin-confronted-neighborhood-watch-volunteer-defense-attorney-says/

[108] Wemple, E. (2012) *Opinion | why did New York Times call George Zimmerman 'white Hispanic'*, Washington Post. Available at: https://www.washingtonpost.com/blogs/erik-wemple/post/why-did-new-york-times-call-george-zimmerman-white-hispanic/2012/03/28/gIQAW6fngS_blog.html

[109] Ball, J. (2015) *'A Short History of Black Lives Matter'—TRNN's Interview with Co-Founder, Patrisse Cullors*, Democratic Underground. Available at: https://www.democraticunderground.com/1017281414

[110] Klein, J. (2020) *BLM founder mentored by Ex-Domestic Terrorist who worked with Bill Ayers*, Breitbart. Available at: https://www.breitbart.com/politics/2020/06/24/

1. *Believes Marxism would make human society better.*
2. *Committed to ending capitalism and replacing it with socialism.*
3. *Dedicated to achieving political power to implement socialism.*
4. *Willing to use violence and revolution to achieve their goals.*[111]

Also, Marxism-Leninism was the preferred method of communism which ruled the old Soviet Union.

The Breitbart story identifies Eric Mann as Ms. Cullors' personal mentor. Mr. Mann was a member of the *Weather Underground*, a group which openly called for the overthrow of the U.S. government and bombed government buildings during the 1960s and 1970s. Mr. Mann mentored Ms. Cullors in community organizing for about 10 years at the *Labor/Community Strategy Center*. The Breitbart article explains the ideology of the Strategy Center as:

> *The center also expresses its appreciation for the work of the U.S. Communist Party, "especially Black communists," as well as its support for "the great work of the Black Panther Party, the American Indian Movement, Young Lords, Brown Berets, and the great revolutionary rainbow experiments of the 1970s," while flaunting its roots in the new communist movement.*

Keep in mind, these are the people who have been embraced by the NEA, entire school districts, and individual teachers/activists across the nation.

---

black-lives-matter-founder-mentored-by-ex-domestic-terrorist-who-worked-with-bill-ayers/

[111] Definition of *Leninism* (2024) *Encyclopædia Britannica*. Available at: https://www.britannica.com/topic/Leninism

Black Lives Matter at School Principles

BLMAS defines itself as a national coalition working for *racial justice in education* guided by thirteen principles.[112] There's the number thirteen again. Probably nothing, but Leftists seem to use thirteen a lot. BLMAS explains their guiding principles with positive and uplifting language, as they always do. However, when you read between the lines, we find strong influences from the *Psychology of Shame*. I won't cover all thirteen, but here are a few selected principles as presented on the BLMAS website (as of 2023):

> *Restorative Justice—As we forge our path, we intentionally cultivate and sustain an environment that is rooted in compassion and empathy, where we can make mistakes, grow, and express the fullness of our humanity.*

It all sounds very nice. It always does. However, you must remember the various justice movements require someone to correct historical wrongs. Social justice, racial justice, climate justice, economic justice, seems like there's a new justice crusade every day and they all have one thing in common. Somehow, you are responsible for historical injustices and they need your money cleanse you of your sins. They also often need to take away your freedoms to ensure you never, ever do it again.

The next principle:

> *Globalism—We recognize that we're part of the global Black family in a common struggle toward liberation. We stay attuned to the different ways we are impacted including our privilege as Black folx who exist in different parts of the world alongside our other contexts.*

---

[112] *13 guiding principles*, BLM at School. Available at: https://www.blacklivesmatteratschool. com/13-guiding-principles.html

First, in this paragraph, BLM spells the world "folks" with an "x." Instead of f-o-l-k-s, they spell it f-o-l-x. To explain the "x," Wellandgood. com says the "x" comes from Leftist efforts to eliminate gender-centered language. For example, Spanish words often have masculine and feminine versions such as Latino and Latina. Leftists see this as a problem in a world where some people identify as neither male nor female. So they invented the word *Latinx* to avoid gender-centered aspects of the Spanish language.[113]

However, the Hispanic community doesn't seem to be embracing Latinx. A YouTube video published in 2021 from *King 5 Seattle*, a television news station, says 77% of all Hispanic adults never heard the term Latinx and only 3% self-identify as Latinx. The video also explains the term was created in the early 2000's by academics, of course.

Only an academic would be stupid enough to believe an entire culture with gender-based language, would abandon that gender-based language to appease less than 1% of the population. A 2021 survey by the Williams Institute from the UCLA School of Law, found 1.2 million U.S citizens identify as non-binary, neither male nor female.[114] That's 0.36% of the U.S. population according to 2024 U.S. Census figures.[115]

Next, the term *Globalism* requires a long explanation. *Globalism* exists as a major component of Leftist thinking. Black Globalists believe Global Socialist Utopia can only exist after the elimination of all individual nation-states. The vision is simple, a world without borders nor capitalism, ruled by one single Marxist government, leads to the best possible future for

---

[113] McPhillips, K. (2021) *What you need to know about the letter 'x' in words like FOLX, Womxn, and latinx, Well+Good.* Available at: https://www.wellandgood.com/folx-meaning/

[114] Wilson, B. and Meyer, I. (2022) *Nonbinary LGBTQ adults in the United States, Williams Institute.* Available at: https://williamsinstitute.law.ucla.edu/publications/nonbinary-lgbtq-adults-us/

[115] *U.S. and World Population Clock, United States Census Bureau.* Available at: https://www.census.gov/popclock/

humanity. Anyone who pays attention to history knows this is complete fantasy. However, Leftists enthusiastically embrace the illusion.

To continue, once Global Socialist Utopia has been achieved, Black radicalists believe they can end all racism by creating a single Black nation-state within a global community. So, in order to end racism, Black Globalists want to eliminate all nation-states and then create a one world government. After eliminating all nation-states, they want to form a brand new, Black-only nation-state populated by every single Black person in the world. If you're having trouble keeping up, don't feel bad. Most Leftist ideologies come with a number of contradicting beliefs.

Marxist academic Mike Cole says only a Global Black Nation will end racism.[116] Dr. Cole believes racism is a global issue which requires a global solution. Dr. Cole defines this Global Black Nation as an all-Black country without borders. Every single Black person on Earth would enjoy citizenship regardless of location.

Dr. Cole explains the idea in his scholarly article titled, *A Marxist Critique of Sean Walton's Defence of the Critical Race Theory Concept of 'White supremacy' as Explaining All Forms of Racism, and Some Comments on Critical Race Theory, Black Radical and Socialist Futures.* Yes, only an academic would be stupid enough to create that title. And yes, he's British. That's why he spells *defense* funny.

In the article, through the lens of *Black Radicalism*, Dr. Cole explains nation-states perpetuate systemic racism. Therefore, they'll never end racism because they desire a racist society. According to Dr. Cole, a true global model serves as the only answer because a Black American has more in common with a Black Kenyan than his White American neighbor. Therefore, Dr. Cole believes White supremacy will only end when Black

---

[116] Cole, M. (2019) *A Marxist critique of Sean Walton's defence of the Critical Race Theory concept of 'White supremacy' as explaining all forms of racism, and some comments on Critical Race Theory, Black Radical and socialist futures, Sage Journals.* Available at: https://journals.sagepub.com/doi/10.1177/1757743819871318

people from all nations around the world unite as one voice and one Global Black Nation. You just know he's become very wealthy peddling this crap. Keep in mind, Marxists are only offended when other people are rich. They don't mind at all when they themselves become rich.

An interesting side note, Marxist academics Mike Cole and Sean Walton spend a great deal of time writing about each other in their scholarly articles. Dr, Cole put Dr. Walton's name right in the title of the article we just discussed. Meanwhile, Dr. Walton cited 13 articles by Dr. Cole in his research paper titled, *Why the Critical Race Theory Concept of 'White Supremacy' Should Not Be Dismissed by Neo-Marxists: Lessons from Contemporary Black Radicalism.* That's another fantastic title, right? Personally, I think Dr. Cole and Dr. Walton have a not-so-secret Marxist man-crush on each other, but that's just my opinion.

Another interesting side note is that Dr. Cole describes *Whiteness* as fluid. We've already discussed *Whiteness*, but let's review it. *Whiteness* defines levels of privilege between races. For example, under *Whiteness*, White people enjoy inherent societal advantages over people of color. However, since *Whiteness* can also be fluid, Dr. Cole says racial privilege also exists between members of non-White groups. Yes, an African American person can enjoy *Whiteness* over another African American person.

The next BLM principle:

> *Trans Affirming—We are self-reflexive and consistently do the work required to dismantle cisgender privilege. We hold space for our siblings who are agender, intersex, transgender, and gender expansive to participate and lead. We uplift Black trans folk, especially Black trans women who continue to be targeted and subjected to violence. We work outside of the binary to achieve full liberation.*

For those who don't know, mirriam-webster.com defines *cisgender* as a person whose gender identify matches their gender identification at birth.[117] If you have a penis, you believe you're male. If you have a vagina, you believe you're female. Additionally, after reading this paragraph, I think it's pretty safe to assume BLMAS lesson plans include "gender-affirming" materials designed to confuse your children.

Moving on to the next BLM principle, as a Marxist organization, BLMAS believes male and female parented nuclear families enable oppressor vs oppressed societies. Therefore, BLMAS commits to disrupting the traditional Western family and advocating for untraditional family units. The principle reads:

> *Black Villages—We disrupt the narrow Western prescribed nuclear family structure expectation. We support each other as extended families and villages that collectively care for one another, especially "our" children. We believe that radical care belongs in the public sphere.*

Notice they refer to your children as "our" children. Marxists always feel entitled to your children. Keep in mind, Marxism sees any organization competing for the people's allegiance as a threat. The nuclear family tops that list. To further explain, the University of Regina in Canada documents the Marxist definition of the family in their Sociology 250 class description.[118]

The curriculum says Friedrich Engels best defined the Marxist view on families in his work titled, *The Origin of the Family, Private Property, and the State*, published in 1884. Engels, one of the recognized fathers of

---

[117] *Cisgender definition & meaning, Merriam-Webster.* Available at: https://www.merriam-webster.com/dictionary/cisgender

[118] *Sociology 250—Introduction to Social Theory* (2002) *Marx on social class, University of Regina.* Available at: https://uregina.ca/~gingrich/o402.htm

Marxism, said the traditional family perpetuates class oppression. Engels believed a truly classless culture can only be realized with the elimination of the family as the basic unit of society. This is the obvious source for BLM's view on families.

The course description also says Karl Marx and Engels blamed the nuclear family for the exploitation of women. They defined women's roles in child-rearing and household management as unpaid labor. Marx believed work shapes consciousness and housework made women think less of themselves, leading to subjugation by men.

Along with eliminating capitalism, Marx and Engels saw a matriarchal society as the solution for eliminating sexism. This might partly explain why the three female BLM founders love Marxism. How might a Marxist matriarchal society look?

According to the *Mises Institute*, Marxism wants to return society to a time when unrestricted sexual intercourse existed between all men and women in a tribe. Engels' writings explain men and women had relationships with multiple partners. When it came to children, only mothers could be unquestionably identified. Therefore, female lineage formed the basis of society and women tended to have ruling authority. Another reason why BLM's female founders might love Marxism.

Engels continues, with the identity of the father always in question, children were raised in extended matriarchal family units called gentes. Hunter and gatherer tribes generally consisted of multiple gentes. Male and female procreative relationships only existed between different gentes to avoid in-breeding. According to Engels, this form of society existed for thousands of years.

Finally, Engels explains, as children's fathers were largely unidentified, in-breeding became more and more difficult to avoid. Pairing families soon emerged with committed male-female relationships. Within faithful relationships, the lineages of both the father and mother could be tracked. The nuclear family soon became the norm.[119] The University of Regina course description continues by saying, from there, stable families led to an agricultural society with planted crops and domesticated animals. Now raising crops and caring for livestock requires private property. Inequality tied to wealth and class soon followed.

So, from the Marxist mindset, the nuclear family must go. However, one difficult problem exists, thriving children often live with two biological parents. Many Leftists argue children fare best in multi-generational families and they should replace the two-parent nuclear household as the norm. This represents a family structure more closely aligned with the gentes so loved by Marx and Engels.

However, the Leftist magazine, *The Atlantic*, admitted the evidence says otherwise. Even in extended families, a loving two-parent household is still the best indicator of a stable childhood. While helpful in child-rearing, grandparents in the home don't make up the difference when one parent is missing. Even bringing in a non-biological substitute, such as a stepfather, can't replicate the success of two married parents.[120] *The Atlantic* article goes on by saying:

> ...*communities are stronger and safer when they include lots of committed married couples. It's good news, then, that the share of children being raised by their own married parents is on the rise. Extended kin can (and sometimes must) play a greater role in meeting children's needs. But as any parent knows, when it comes to an inconsolable child, even a "dozen pairs of arms" from*

[119] Thomas, B. (2020) *Why Marxist organizations like BLM seek to dismantle the 'Western Nuclear Family'*, Mises Institute. Available at: https://mises.org/wire/why-marxist-organizations-blm-seek-dismantle-western-nuclear-family

[120] Boyd, H. and Wilcox, B. (2020) *The nuclear family is still indispensable*, The Atlantic. Available at: https://www.theatlantic.com/ideas/archive/2020/02/nuclear-family-still-indispensable/606841/

the village don't quite compare to the warm and safe embrace of Mom or Dad.

One final point, *The Atlantic* also references a 2001 *Cornell Law Review* study which shows female children in non-traditional families are significantly more likely to suffer from sexual abuse and all children are more likely suffer from all forms of abuse when living with non-biological parents.[121] This is not new information.

Black Lives Matter Money

The Claremont Institute Center for the American Way of Life attempted to track BLM fund-raising and spending in early 2023. As grudgingly reported by the "journalists" at *Newsweek*, BLM raised or received pledges for almost $83 billion dollars from corporations and companies from 2020 to 2023.[122] While only $123 million can be directly traced to BLM's parent organization, the article notes BLM is coordinated from the top, but only loosely organized at the local level. This can often be a recipe for corruption. *Newsweek* then admits these numbers, "*likely underrepresent the true magnitude of the shakedown as many companies failed to make known their contributions.*"

The Epoch Times notes top corporate donors include JP Morgan Chase, Bank of America, Goldman Sachs, Starbucks, Citigroup, PNC Financial Services, Facebook, New York Life Insurance, BlackRock, CVS Health, PayPal, Mastercard, Pepsi, Google, IBM, the NFL, Microsoft, Netflix, and

[121] Wilson, R.F. (2001) *Children at Risk: The Sexual Exploitation of Female Children after Divorce*, Cornell Law Review, January 2001. Available at: https://scholarship.law.cornell.edu/cgi/viewcontent.cgi?article=2832&context=clr

[122] Claremont Institute Center for the American Way of Life (2023) *Americans deserve to know who funded BLM riots*, Newsweek. Available at: https://www.newsweek.com/americans-deserve-know-who-funded-blm-riots-opinion-1787460

Amazon among many, many others.[123] Of the groups listed here, most donations were for billions or hundreds of millions of dollars.

Where is all this money going? *Newsweek* admits the spending is hard to track and most of it remains unaccountable. However, both *Newsweek* and *The Epoch Times* note BLM destroyed 200 American cities during the summer of 2020 resulting in approximately $2 billion in property damage. Since much of this destruction occurred in minority neighborhoods, it seems the right thing for BLM to do should be to rebuild those communities. However, this hasn't happened yet.

Of the spending that can be traced, top funded initiatives included defunding police departments, promoting CRT curricula in schools, funding election campaigns for like-minded activists, and spending for personal gain. Remember, Marxists always hate rich people, but ironically are never offended by being wealthy themselves. The same article from *The Epoch Times* also detailed the first public accounting of BLM's finances in 2022 which included:

1. *Shalomyah Bowers, head of the BLM Global Network Foundation, allegedly stole over $10 million claiming it was for "front line work."*

2. *According to 2022 tax forms, Ms. Bowers also paid herself over $2 million for "consulting" during 2020 and 2021.*

3. *BLM co-founder Patrisse Cullors purchased a Los Angeles home for $5.8 million with BLM money. Within a week, the title of that home was transferred to a Delaware LLC without identifying the new owner.*

---

[123] Athrappully, N. (2023) *American companies poured over $82 billion into black lives matter movement: Think tank, The Epoch Times.* Available at: https://www.theepochtimes. com/american-companies-poured-over-82-billion-into-black-lives-matter-movement-think-tank_5127646.html

4. *Ms. Cullors paid $840,000 to her brother's security company.*

5. *Ms. Cullors also paid the father of her child, Damon Turner, almost $1 million for "cultural architecture."*

Now this is about the time *Reader's Digest* came to the rescue. After the initial money scandals broke, *Reader's Digest* published multiple articles detailing where you can safely donate money to BLM and its related causes with peace of mind. The *Reader's Digest's* stated purpose behind the article? They were worried about BLM copycat organizations siphoning money away from the genuine movement. The real purpose? BLM had been outed as a terrible steward of charity dollars and donations slowed down.

In these articles, *Reader's Digest* provided a list of worthy BLM causes including BLM itself. Often they included "support now" buttons below the charity descriptions. At the same time, *Reader's Digest* admitted only a fraction of BLM donations trickle down to African American communities.[124] If you ever needed absolute proof BLM is a Marxist organization, this is it. According to all the evidence, BLM kept most of the donations for themselves and gave very little to its intended recipients…poor African Americans. The other lesson here. Perhaps you should reconsider your subscription to *Reader's Digest* if you have one.

Just a few months later, the *New York Post* published an op-ed titled, *BLM's Financial Fall Proves It Only Used Dead Black People to Cash In*.[125] Ouch. The article read:

---

[124] Foster, S. (2023) *55 BLM charities (and organizations) to donate to right now, Reader's Digest*. Available at: https://www.rd.com/article/black-lives-matter-donate/

[125] Coleman, A.B. (2023) *BLM's financial fall proves it only used dead black people to cash in, New York Post*. Available at: https://nypost.com/2023/05/29/blms-financial-fall-proves-it-only-used-dead-black-people-to-cash-in/

> *... we don't expect the leaders of a charity that claims moral righteousness to immorally use their donations to live amongst the 1% while pretending to benefit the 13% of black Americans....at the very least, if it's going to say it's trying to help black people, it should actually do it.*

Returning to the *Reader's Digest*, to continue their effort to make you feel better about giving money to people with questionable financial and personal integrity, the magazine explained BLM partnered with *Thousand Currents* to oversee donations after the money scandals. With *Thousand Currents* in charge of the finances, the *Reader's Digest* claimed, "...*you can donate without worrying where your money is going.*"[126]

Let's look at *Thousand Currents*, shall we? In 2020, the *Capital Research Center* outed Susan Rosenberg, then Vice Chair of the *Thousand Currents* Board of Directors, for her past ties to the *Weather Underground* and the *May 19th Communist Organization*. Both groups have histories of terrorist bombings in New York and Washington, D.C. Remember the radical Marxist-Leninist principles? They believe violence is an acceptable tool to achieve their political gains.

Specifically, Ms. Rosenberg was arrested in 1984 in New Jersey when caught with 740 pounds of stolen explosives and a fully automatic machine gun. Marxists only hate guns when you have them. That same year, she was on the *FBI's Most Wanted List* for her involvement in a bombing campaign protesting President Ronald Reagan's re-election. Ms. Rosenberg also allegedly participated in the 1981 Brink's robbery resulting in the death of two police officers and one security guard; however, she was never charged in that crime.[127]

---

[126] Foster, S. (2023) *55 BLM charities (and organizations) to donate to right now, Reader's Digest.* Available at: https://www.rd.com/article/black-lives-matter-donate/

[127] Walter, S. (2020) *A terrorist's ties to a leading Black Lives Matter Group,* Capital Research Center. Available at: https://capitalresearch.org/

Ms. Rosenberg got out of prison in 2001 after President Bill Clinton commuted her sentence on his way out of office. Even Leftists spoke out against that one. The lesson learned here, just because you're a terrorist and a possible murderer, doesn't mean you can't make a nifty financial advisor. Usually, when something like Ms. Rosenberg's past come out, Marxists batten down the hatches and just try to ride out the storm with the help of a sympathetic media. But Ms. Rosenberg's history was just too much. *Thousand Currents* removed her from their Board of Directors in 2020.

If we look at *Thousand Currents'* 2023 Board of Directors advertised on their website, we don't see anyone as bad as Ms. Rosenberg. I'm not going to bore you with a complete rundown, but every single member has some form of "justice" on their resume. Racial justice, social justice, environmental justice, land justice, housing justice, and climate justice among others. As already discussed, Leftists are always inventing new forms of "justice."

While not on the Board of Directors, one team member listed on *Thousand Currents* website is a woman named Sarah Charles. The interesting thing about her resume, she previously worked for George Soros's radical *Open Society Foundations*. In January 2023, the *New York Post* called George Soros the most dangerous man in America.[128]

The Post says Mr. Soros spends tens of millions of dollars installing Leftist District Attorneys (DA) in major cities across the country. These DA's then implement "crime reforms" which protect criminals and lead to sky-rocketing crime rates. The Post article continues by saying Mr. Soros also pays various media personalities and "fact checkers" to convince everyone the surging crime rates are not really happening. My personal opinion, Ms. Charles probably still works for Mr. Soros, in some capacity, as she goes about daily tasks at *Thousand Currents*.

---

article/a-terrorists-ties-to-a-leading-black-lives-matter-group/

[128] *George Soros is the most dangerous man in America–here's why* (2023) *New York Post.* Available at: https://nypost.com/2023/01/26/ george-soros-is-the-most-dangerous-man-in-america-heres-why/

Black Lives Matter at School and Learning for Justice

National educational leaders love to deny CRT exists in American schools and they also love to voice support for BLM and BLMAS. However, like most things related to CRT, we find another unexplainable contradiction. BLMAS educational materials come from an organization called, *Learning for Justice* (LFJ), which openly admits their classroom resources contain CRT. Just in case you haven't noticed, *Learning for Justice* includes another reference to the word "justice."

If we go the LFJ website, we find pre-prepared CRT lesson plans and professional development courses.[129] On the very first page, under the *Classroom Resources* dropdown menu, we find a lesson titled, *'Bibi' Lesson 2: Intersectionality in 'Bibi.'* You may remember *intersectionality* is a primary CRT tenet defined as the multiplied effects of racism, sexism, classism, etc.[130] Selections from the course description say:

> In this second of three lessons on the film 'Bibi,' students will apply the concepts of intersectionality, privilege and oppression to characters from the film.

> Explain that the way people interact with each other can also be based on the idea of oppression. This is the idea that a minority identity group can be systematically exploited, degraded, or harmed by a dominant identity group.

> Lead the class in summarizing how your identity characteristics intersect to create unique forms of privilege or oppression.

---

[129]Lessons (2020) *Learning for Justice*, Southern Poverty Law Center. Available at: https://www.learningforjustice.org/classroom-resources/lessons

[130]Jones, A. M. (2021). *Conflicted: How African American women negotiate their responses to racial microaggressions at a historically white institution, Race Ethnicity and Education.* Available at: https://doi.org/10.1080/13613324.2021.1924136

Hopefully, by now, you're recognizing CRT code words and phrases, such as *privilege, oppression, systemically exploited, dominant identity group,* etc. Again, just because you don't see the words "Critical Race Theory," doesn't mean the lesson isn't packed with CRT concepts.

To reinforce these theories, the lesson calls for students to watch a video titled, *Intersectionality 101.* I've provided a hyperlink to the video below. If you choose to watch it, it's only three minutes long.[131] The video features three characters. Jerry is a handicapped young man of color. He's the oldest of ten children and often provides caregiving for his siblings. His family lives below the poverty line. No guidance counselors have spoken to Jerry about his future after high school. He's applied for a number of jobs, but never gets hired. In the video, a door slams in his face.

Next, we have Fatima. She's Muslim and a recent immigrant from Somalia. Fatima says her fellow students make assumptions about her before getting to know her better. At this point, the video shows three angry faces of other students and the words, "Go Away!" Remember the *Psychology of Shame* from *Wit & Wisdom?* The video then says, *"Many of her classmates think she shouldn't be at their school at all."*

Finally, we have a White girl named Greta. Greta's family owns a successful business and both parents attended college. She sees herself following in her parents' footsteps. The video says Greta doesn't often consider her identity due to her privilege. Overall, the video portrays Greta's life as one without challenges. Meanwhile, identity and intersectionality affect Jerry and Fatima every single day. The video concludes by saying that learning about our identities helps us understand the institutions that *"harm us based on who we are."*

The closing credits show an organization called *Teaching Tolerance Magazine* produced the program. The credits also show *Teaching Tolerance*

---

[131] Learning for Justice (2016) *Intersectionality 101, YouTube.* Available at: https://www. youtube.com/watch?v=w6dnj2IyYjE

is a project of the *Southern Poverty Law Center* (SPLC). If we go to SPLC's webpage, the *About Us* section reads:[132]

> The SPLC is a catalyst for racial justice in the South and beyond, working in partnership with communities to dismantle white supremacy, strengthen intersectional movements, and advance the human rights of all people.

As you can see, we find wall-to-wall CRT code words including the word *"justice"* which generally means give us your money so you can feel better about injustices you never committed. If the SPLC is like many Leftist organizations, any donations sent to them may never leave the building.

PRIMARY LESSONS: Critical Race Theory has permeated our entire society. Our most familiar brands push it every day. According to *The Epoch Times*, the largest donors to BLM and its related causes were some of the most well-known brand names in the world.[133]

Remember, this is just their donations to one group…BLM and its related causes. How many other similar groups exist? If we count the money that can tracked, they donated almost $83 billion dollars supporting BLM which is *"more than the combined GDP of 46 African nations,"* according to *The Epoch Times*.

What can we do about it? It's tough. I boycotted Starbucks a long time ago over things like ignoring police officers trying to buy coffee.[134] When Netflix streamed the disgusting program, *Cuties*, which sexualized

---

[132] *About Us, Southern Poverty Law Center*. Available at: https://www.splcenter.org/about

[133] Athrappully, N. (2023) *American companies poured over $82 billion into black lives matter movement: Think tank, The Epoch Times*. Available at: https://www.theepochtimes.com/us/american-companies-poured-over-82-billion-into-black-lives-matter-movement-think-tank-5127646

[134] Ortiz, J. (2019) *Starbucks apologizes for third 'anti police' incident in six months, this time in California, USA Today*. Available at:

11-year-old girls, I stopped my subscription.[135] When DirecTV removed NewsMax from their channel lineup to silence conservative voices, I canceled my service.[136]

But again, it's tough. I'm personally neck deep in Google and Amazon services. You may have noticed I sell this book on Amazon because it's the No.1 book seller in the world. Tough to move on from that if you're a first-time, self-published author like myself. My most used credit card with airline miles comes from JP Morgan Chase and it's been helpful. I've taken several free flights using only my credit card miles over the last few years.

I wrote this book using Microsoft Word because it's my "comfort" word processer. For years, I've used CVS as my pharmacy. Also, I don't think I can live without watching the New York Giants embarrass themselves week after week on television using the NFL Package, previously on DirecTV and now on YouTube TV. Google owns YouTube. And my year-long Netflix boycott ended when it was the only streaming service with a program I really, really wanted to watch. However, my Netflix boycott has since been reinstated. Like I said, it's tough and we are all weak when it comes to moving out of our comfort zones.

However, I suppose I should set the example here. The best thing to do is start with the easiest boycotts. With that in mind, I pledge to change my pharmacy. Next, I found a new word processer and publishing software called *Atticus* which I will use to write my next book. I also re-quit my Netflix subscription as I just mentioned and paid for Proton Mail to

---

https://www.usatoday.com/story/news/nation/2019/12/15/starbucks-offers-apology-completely-ignored-california-deputies/2658767001/

[135] Nash, C. (2020) '#cancelnetflix': Service faces boycott after 'Cuties' scene sexualizing children goes viral, Mediaite. Available at: https://www.mediaite.com/entertainment/cancelnetflix-streaming-service-faces-new-calls-for-boycott-after-cuties-scene-sexualizing-children-goes-viral/

[136] AT&T's DIRECTV Cancels Newsmax in censorship move (2023) Newsmax. Available at: https://www.newsmax.com/newsfront/newsmax-at-t-directv/2023/01/24/id/1105756/

begin moving away from Google services. Remember, if something is free, YOU are the product. You should begin considering ways you can fight back against woke companies.

The good thing about canceling DirecTV, I was able to call and tell them why I was quitting. The nice lady on the phone began offering many great deals, but I held firm. When I re-quit Netflix, their website gave me the opportunity to explain why. I told them it was because of their "woke agenda."

If you get an opportunity to tell a "woke" company why you're leaving, do it. In the meantime, try to spend your dollars somewhere else. It's not always easy to do. If you cancelled every video streaming service with a woke agenda, would you be able to subscribe to any of them at all? Probably not. However, one change was fairly easy. I love small, independent coffee houses and they make excellent coffee…even better than Starbucks.

CHAPTER SEVEN

TEACHER TRAINING AND INDOCTRINATION

Introduction

OUR EDUCATORS GET bombarded with woke indoctrination. California's Ethnic Studies Model Curriculum (CESMC) provides a perfect example. Students must pass CESMC to graduate, teachers must teach it, and state administrators plan to spread CRT concepts into every single class your child attends.

The teachers' unions push CRT, countless educational organizations push CRT, textbooks push CRT, and required teacher trainings push CRT as well. Everywhere teachers look, they find CRT embedded in their educational resources.

That doesn't excuse the misguided instructors who enthusiastically try to indoctrinate your children, but it helps to understand the pressures good teachers face, and the resistance they receive when they try to take a stand.

San Diego Unified School District and Spirit Murdering

In 2020, the San Diego Unified School District (SDUSD) hired a well-known CRT supporter, Dr. Bettina Love, to conduct *anti-racist* and *social justice* training for teachers. At the beginning of the training, SDUSD told teachers that recording the training sessions was forbidden. Unfortunately for them, the training was conducted virtually. A whistleblower doc-umented the sessions and offered the content to Christopher Rufo, an anti-CRT scholar at the *Discovery Institute*. Mr. Rufo then shared the information on *Twitter/X*. The Tweets read:

> SCOOP: *San Diego Unified School District tells white teachers they are guilty of "spirit murdering" black children and should undergo "antiracist therapy for White educators." I've obtained explosive whistleblower documents from the training session. Let's dig in.*

> *This summer, San Diego Unified hired critical race theorist Bettina Love for a district-wide training on "[challenging] the oppressive practices that live within ... school organizations." The district forbade recordings, but my whistleblower took screenshots and detailed notes.*

> *According to the whistleblower notes, Love began by saying that "racism runs deep" in America and that blacks alone "know who America really is." Love claimed that public schools "don't see [blacks] as human," perpetuate "anti-Blackness," and "spirit murder babies."*

> *The concept of "spirit murder" is at the heart of Love's teachings. Love writes that public schools are guilty of "the spirit murdering of Black and Brown children," defines as "a death that is built on racism and intended to reduce, humiliate, and destroy people of color."*[137]

---

[137] Rufo, C.F. (2021) *According to the whistleblower notes, Love began by saying that 'Racism runs deep' in America and that blacks alone 'Know who america really is.' Love claimed that public schools 'don't see [blacks] as human,' perpetuate 'anti-blackness,' and 'Spirit*

Let's look more closely at Dr. Love's background. Her past scholarly works are filled with extremely divisive ideas. After reading Mr. Rufo's Tweets, that should come as no surprise. Statements such as, *"Black children are dehumanized and criminalized from the moment they enter those school doors,"* are common.

Here's a selection from a research paper written by Dr. Love titled, *Anti-Black state violence, classroom edition: The spirit murdering of Black children.* It's rather long, but it's important to read the entire excerpt in my opinion. It says:

> *I want to draw attention to how school officials like Gordeuk and Fields—regardless of their race, gender, or ethnicity—"spirit murder" the souls of Black children every day through systemic, institutionalized, anti-Black, state-sanctioned violence. That intangible violence toward Black children is less visceral and seemingly less tragic than the physical acts of murder at the hands of White mobs, kidnapping and killing by White self-appointed vigilantes, or shootings by police officers in their homes and streets. But a slow death, a death of the spirit, is a death that is built on racism and intended to "humiliate, reduce, and destroy." Racism is indelible to the Black body and the spirit, and the physical and spirit murdering of Black bodies is unfortunately part-and-parcel of America's history. It is, in many ways, what makes America, America.*[138]

To explain the names Gordeuk and Fields, according to Dr. Love's paper, Georgia principal Nancy Gordeuk dismissed a high school graduation

---

murder babies.' pic.twitter.com/jummapxz79, Twitter. Available at: https://twitter.com/realchrisrufo/status/1346852356521037825

[138] Love, B.L. (2016) *The spirit murdering of black children,* bettinalove.com. Available at: https://bettinalove.com/wp-content/uploads/2018/09/Anti-Black-state-violence-classroom-edition-The-spirit-murdering-of-Black-children.pdf

ceremony before the valedictorian gave his or her speech. Principal Gordeuk tried to call everyone back, but most continued to leave. Principal Gordeuk then allegedly said, *"Look who's leaving…all the Black people."*

Then we have South Carolina high school Security Officer Ben Fields, who tossed a young African American girl across the room for refusing to obey instructions. Two other students videoed the incident and tried to present their evidence to school officials. In response, administrators arrested one of the student whistleblowers for *"disturbing the school."* The investigation later revealed Mr. Fields had a history of overly aggressive behavior.

Obviously, there's no defending the actions of either individual, assuming Dr. Love's paper accurately depicted both situations. Remember, as a CRT supporter, Dr. Love most likely encourages counter-storytelling, the CRT tenet that approves of narratives with all, some, or none of the truth.

For the sake of argument, let's assume Dr. Love's accounts of the Gordeuk and Fields incidents are completely true. Dr. Love believes this behavior reveals a national trend of systemic racism. She also thinks White supremacists work to cover up that widespread racism and pretend it doesn't exist. In her paper, Dr. Love says, *"The media would like to portray these incidents as isolated, the work of a few racist, overzealous, culturally insensitive school officials."*

From a different perspective, in a nation of 336 million+ people, you're going to have bad actors, but they do not drive national trends. Dr. Love mentions Mike Brown and Trayvon Martin in her article. I also mentioned both men earlier in this book. If you remember, both young men engaged in violence against others before losing their lives and were then portrayed as innocent victims in the press.

If we want to take Dr. Love's assertions and turn them around, should we apply her logic about the Gordeuk and Fields incidents to Mr. Brown's and Mr. Martin's tragic happenings? For example, should we assume all young men of color are violent because Mr. Brown and Mr. Martin attacked others just before their lives ended? Does this call for a systemic approach to the problem such as anti-violence classes for all young men of color? Of course not, that would be ridiculous, but that's the kind of logic we can expect from CRT supporters like Dr. Love.

Looking at Dr. Love's work reveals her long history with this type of rhetoric. Dr. Love's 2019 op-ed titled, *How Schools Are 'Spirit Murdering' Black and Brown Students,*[139] includes selections such as:

> *In Binghamton, N.Y., four 12-year-old Black girls reported they were strip-searched at their school for acting too hyper and giddy in January. School officials likely assumed the girls were on drugs because their Black joy was unrecognizable*

A few sentences later, Dr. Love admits "strip searched" meant school officials removed some of the girls' clothing, but doesn't define "some." Does that mean school officials had the girls remove an outer winter coat or sweater? Or did they inappropriately remove more? We don't know. Also, we don't know why Dr. Love assumes the school officials "likely" believed the girls were on drugs. Is this a counter-story? How much is true? All? Some? Or none?

This Dr. Love article appeared in *Education Week*. Keep in mind, *Education Week* is one of the most respected educational journals in the nation. Hard to believe they kept their reputation intact after publishing this story. Dr. Love also authored two books titled, *We Want to do More Than Survive* and *Punished for Dreaming*. By now, I think you understand Dr. Love.

---

[139] Love, B.L. (2023) *How schools are 'spirit murdering' black and brown students (opinion), Education Week.* Available at: https://www.edweek.org/leadership/opinion-how-schools-are-spirit-murdering-black-and-brown-students/2019/05

An interesting trend among extreme Leftists such as Dr. Love, they tend to receive countless awards and accolades. She's a visiting professor at Columbia University, she was named the *Nasir Jones HipHop Fellow* at Harvard University, the Kennedy Center called her one of the *Next 50 Leaders* dedicated to making the world more compassionate, *Education Week* ranked her as No. 40 on their *Edu-Scholar Public Influence Ranking* list in 2022 (No. 113 in 2021), she's a visiting scholar at the University of Pittsburgh, she's a scholar-in-residence at the University of Houston, the Georgia State University Alumni Association recognized her as one of their top *40 Under 40* persons, and the Georgia House of Representatives presented her with a resolution honoring her impact on the field of education.[140] Not bad for a woman who accuses all White teachers of spirit murdering Black and Brown students.

How does a person with such divisive work garner so much recognition? Easy. Leftists love giving each other awards. It makes their extreme ideas seem acceptable to the masses. A parent who is only half paying attention might say, she sure sounds crazy, but the state of Georgia recognized her as one of the best in education. That must mean something. Dr. Love even sells her own *merch* to further influence the people.[141]

I never saw any direct evidence Dr. Love is a Marxist, other than her love of CRT and BLM, until I saw her merchandise page. Her T-shirts cost an outrageously expensive $32 if you can believe it and her official store policy is "**ALL SALES ARE FINAL. NO RETURNS OR EXCHANGES**." Very authoritarian. Once she gets your money, she never gives it back. Yep, all signs point to her being a true Marxist.

---

[140] *Bio* (2024) *Bettina Love.* Available at: https://bettinalove.com/bio/

[141] *Shop* (2024) *Bettina Love.* Available at: https://bettinalove.com/shop/

Californians for Equal Rights Foundation v. San Diego Unified School District

The Californians for Equal Rights Foundation (CFER) eventually filed a civil rights complaint against SDUSD for Dr. Love's training, among other things. The complaint, titled *For Unlawful Racial Discrimination in the Teacher & Staff Training Process*, claimed the school district engaged in discriminatory, biased, and hostile training programs against its employees. Beyond Dr. Love's training, the CFER complaint also encompassed three other similar mandatory training programs which occurred during 2020.[142]

First, the complaint details training called, *White Privilege: Understanding Power and Privilege in Education*. Similar to Dr. Love's training sessions, the course materials focused heavily on "oppressive White power" in San Diego's schools and how it prevents academic success for Black children.

The course included three lessons called *Examining White Privilege*, *Exploring Aspects of Privilege and White Culture*, and *White Privilege in the Classroom*. Attendees watched videos from well-known anti-racists, such as Ibram X. Kendi, and were then told, "you are racist" and accused them of upholding "racist ideas, structures, and policies." Teachers were also told they must become anti-racist activists in their classrooms by confronting their White privilege.

The course materials also made numerous unsupported claims. They included statements such as *"drivers are less likely to stop for Blacks in a crosswalk then whites," "2/3 of Black Americans say they are treated less well while shopping than Whites,"* and *"67% of doctors have a bias against Blacks."* If these things were true, there would be peer-reviewed academic research proving it to be true. You can also be sure the "trainers" would've presented that evidence during the training to support their assertions. They did not.

---

[142] *Complaint of Californians for Equal Rights Foundation v. San Diego Unified School District for unlawful racial discrimination in the teacher & staff training process* (2021) media. graphassets.com. Available at: https://media.graphassets.com/C5tF87U6Sbe1bKcvGv5e

The second training program mentioned in the CFER complaint is titled *Anti-Racist Leaders* from SDUSD's *Anti-Racist Leadership Summer Camp.* The facilitators were Dr. Dulcinea Hearn and Ms. Ebonee Weathers, two African American Vernacular English (AAVE) experts. *Dictionary. com* defines AAVE as Black English, distinctly different from Standard American English, which originated with Black slaves from Pre-Civil War southern plantations. In 1996, the Oakland, California school board recognized AAVE as the native language of 30,000 African American students within the school district.[143]

CFER claims the training materials for the *Anti-Racist Training* course clearly promoted CRT among San Diego's teachers. In one example, Dr. Hearn and Ms. Weathers used a counter-story, one of the primary tenets of CRT, which again may include all, some, or none of the truth. The facilitators told the counter-story of one teacher who stopped an anti-Black racist joke before it happened. According to the story, the teacher "sensed" a racist joke was about to happen and shut down the alleged perpetrator before they said one word. Dr. Hearn and Ms. Weathers referred to this action as *interrupting racism.* Trainees were also encouraged to interrupt racism on social media by drowning out voices who disagreed with Black Lives Matter.

Additionally, Dr. Hearn and Ms. Weathers introduced the concept of *anti-bias, anti-racism* (ABAR). Under ABAR, teachers were encouraged to use their classrooms as reeducation camps to promote anti-racist activism. Are you seeing a trend here?

The third example from the CFER complaint, a training course named, *Critical Self Awareness: An Intro into Anti-Racist Pedagogy. Merriam-Webster. com* defines pedagogy as the art and profession of teaching.[144] In this

---

[143]Khera, T. (2021) *The complexity of African American Vernacular English,* Dictionary.com. Available at: https://www.dictionary.com/e/ united-states-diversity-african-american-vernacular-english-aave/

[144]*Pedagogy definition & meaning,* Merriam-Webster. Available at: https://www.merriam-webster.com/dictionary/pedagogy

training, teachers were taught how to become anti-racist activists. For White teachers, becoming an anti-racist involved accepting their White privilege and working to undo their inherent racism. For African American teachers, being an anti-racist meant understanding the ways in which they appease racism and learning new methods to stop racism. The facilitators also claimed racism directed at White and Black people have very different outcomes. According to the training, racism against White people generally has no long-lasting effects. However, racism against African American people often results in negative life-altering social and economic consequences.

From a legal perspective, the CFER complaint said this training violated state and federal anti-discrimination laws. CFER referred to Title VII of the Civil Rights Act of 1964, as well as the California Education Code and San Diego School Board policy. Each law and/or policy says employers may not discriminate against anyone based on race. To support this premise, CFER quoted U.S. Civil Rights Commissioner Peter Kirsanow from a letter in August 2020, who said this type of anti-racist training doesn't reduce racism, it creates more. Mr. Kirsanow's letter said:

> *There is no way that separating white employees from other employees and telling them that this grab-bag of characteristics are inherent to white people and are bad (and therefore, that they have these characteristics and are bad) does not adversely affect their status in the eyes of their co-workers. The obverse also is true. This juvenile grouping of terms necessarily stereotypes non-whites too.*

I reached out to CFER in November 2023 for the latest on their complaint. A CFER representative said SDUSD is dragging out the case, originally filed in April 2021, by conducting its own investigation before addressing the CFER complaint. My initial thought? Why does it take two years to decide if "spirit murdering" is an appropriate training subject for teachers? CFER also defined their civil rights complaint against SDUSD as an administrative procedure and not a lawsuit.

PRIMARY LESSON: In extreme cases, you may need to take legal or civil action against your school or district. You can expect a long, expensive fight. Look for local, like-minded organizations such as the Californians for Equal Rights Foundation (CFER) who may be willing to help and/ or provide guidance. Perhaps you can start your own advocacy group but understand this will require a great deal of time and fundraising.

CHAPTER EIGHT

DEFENDING CRITICAL RACE THEORY

Introduction

LEFTISTS WORK HARD at defending CRT, while claiming at the same time, it doesn't exist. Also, their defense strategies often include conflicting messages and weak justifications. These are very common themes we've visited many times in this book. However, this doesn't mean we can't learn from their tactics. Leftists are very good at defending the indefensible and they've been doing it for a very long time.

Again, despite claims K-12 schools definitely do not teach CRT, the *Education Justice Research and Organizing Collaborative* (EJROC), felt the need to create an organizing toolkit to defend CRT. Based at New York University Steinhardt (NYUS), EJROC titled the toolkit, *Winning Racial Justice in Our Schools: Resisting the Right Wing Attacks on Critical Race Theory*. There's the word "justice" again and at least they had the courage to use the words "Critical Race Theory" this time. From the second paragraph of the Organizing Toolkit (OTK):

> ...the Right is amping up their racist strategies – and their newest tactic is attacking critical race theory (CRT)...to eliminate any teaching about systemic racism in schools...They're attacking diversity, equity, and inclusion...most importantly for the Right,

*droves of angry white parents are getting mobilized for the mid-
term elections to take back Congress. Their efforts has been conceived by former Trump strategists, funded by billionaire donors
throwing tens of millions of dollars at the misinformation campaign, and managed by some of the same right-wing organizations
driving racist voter suppression laws across the country.*[145]

I'm pretty sure they hit every single Leftist-trigger-word in existence
in that paragraph. Again, I hope you've learned to recognize them and
their associated concepts by now. Just for fun, my list of Leftist code
words in this paragraph includes *racist strategies, eliminate teaching systemic
racism, attacking diversity, equity, and inclusion, droves of angry white parents,
TRUMP (gasp!!!!), billionaire donors, misinformation campaign, right-wing
organizations,* and *racist voter suppression laws.*

The EJROC would never consider that parents like you are just plain
concerned about your children's education. No, you are an angry, White,
racist mob capable of violence at any given moment, even if you don't
happen to belong to the Caucasian race. There's a reason why Leftist organizations use these name-calling tactics when defending their indefensible
plans and strategies. They work.

Leftists tend to define their opposition as well-organized, well-funded,
and well-connected. When, in fact, they are the ones who are well-organized, well-funded, and well-connected. They use a laundry list of trigger
code words to rile up average citizens and, unfortunately, many of these
well-meaning people believe them.

Let's look at the background of NYUS and EJROC which are two
highly-respected educational institutions. NYUS partners with the

[145] *Winning racial justice in our schools: Resisting the right wing attacks on
Critical Race Theory: Organizing Toolkit* (2021) Education Justice Research
and Organizing Collaborative. Available at: https://static1.squarespace.
com/static/5bc5da7c3560c36b7dab1922/t/6126241c56874d431487
6f6a/1629889575567/CRT+Toolkit+FINAL+August+2021.pdf

United Nations, the China Institute, the Rockefeller Foundation, the American Federation of Teachers, the National Education Association, and the Lincoln Center, among many others.[146] How many of you partner with the United Nations and the National Education Association? Not too many I imagine.

One particular organization on that list, the China Institute, has a very disturbing history. The China Institute funds something called Confucius Institutes at American universities.[147] The federal government believes Confucius Institutes work for the Chinese Communist Party to promote anti-American, pro-Chinese policies and spy on Chinese nationals attending school in the U.S.[148]

The General Accountability Office (GAO) reports the Trump Administration investigated Confucius Institutes and, in 2018, began restricting funding to U.S. schools with hosted institutes. At the time, about 100 Confucius Institutes operated on American campuses. By 2019, only five remained.[149]

The American Spectator reported U.S. universities accepted at least $315 million in donations from Chinese state-owned organizations between 2014 and 2019. $88 million was directly connected to Chinese military defense contractors who engage in cyberattacks against the U.S.

[146] Partners Metropolitan Center for Research on Equity and the transformation of schools (2024) NYU Steinhardt. Available at: https://steinhardt.nyu.edu/metrocenter/about/partners

[147] Confucius Institute at China Institute, China Institute. Available at: https://web.archive.org/web/20220123024223/https://www.chinainstitute.org/about-us/confucius-institute-at-china-institute-cici/

[148] Flatley, D. and Lorin, J. (2023) All but five confucius institutes on US campuses have closed, according to GAO, Bloomberg.com. Available at: https://www.bloomberg.com/news/articles/2023-11-02/china-s-confucius-institutes-are-disappearing-from-us-campuses?leadSource=uverify+wall

[149] China: With nearly all U.S. Confucius Institutes closed, some schools sought alternative language support (2023) U.S. Government Accountability Office. Available at: https://www.gao.gov/products/gao-24-105981

and reverse engineer stolen American military technology such as the F-35 fighter jet.[150]

The *American Spectator* also lists NYU as seventh on the list of universities accepting Chinese money ($56.7 million). The top six were (in order) Harvard, Yale, Stanford, Penn, MIT, and Columbia, which might partially explain the Leftist garbage coming out of our "most prestigious" schools. Furthermore, the *American Spectator* reports many U.S. colleges and universities fail to report billions of dollars in foreign donations, so these numbers are likely just the tip of the iceberg. But parents fighting against CRT are the ones who are well-funded and well-connected, right?

Meanwhile, Leftists like to pretend their favorite activist organizations are grassroots institutions. *Dictionary.com* defines a grassroots organization as a group created by average citizens, not by upper-level, well-funded, well-connected leaders.[151] In other words, they try to convince the public that their members are average, noble citizens inspired to support an honorable cause. As we shall soon learn, when it comes to groups supporting CRT, nothing could be further from the truth. Now let's unpack the tactics used by Leftist groups to defend CRT and their other "honorable" causes.

Saul Alinsky's Rules for Radicals

To better understand the EJROC, we must first consider Saul Alinsky's Leftist-bible, *Rules for Radicals*. Hillary Clinton's thesis at Wellesley College (WELLS-lee) was titled, *THERE IS ONLY THE FIGHT...An Analysis of the Alinsky Model.*[152] President Barack Obama openly admired

[150]Postal, S. (2021) *How the CCP infiltrates American Universities: They've given millions of dollars in undisclosed donations*, The American Spectator | USA News and Politics. Available at: https://spectator.org/ccp-american-universities-confucius-institutes/

[151]*Grassroots definition & usage examples* (no date) Dictionary.com. Available at: https://www.dictionary.com/browse/grassroots

[152]*Hillary Clinton's 1969 thesis on Saul Alinsky: "THERE IS ONLY THE FIGHT..." An Analysis of the Alinsky Model* (2013) EconomicPolicyJournal.com. Available at: https://www.economicpolicyjournal.com/2013/04/hillary-clintons-1969-thesis-on-saul.html

and implemented Mr. Alinsky's teachings while community organizing in Chicago during his younger years.[153]

One can argue, President Obama and Mrs. Clinton were the two most influential Democrats of the last two decades, at least until the 2020 election. Regardless, Saul Alinsky's strategies endure. Some believe he's more relevant now than he was 50 years ago when he died.

In *Rules for Radicals*, Mr. Alinsky created a 13-step playbook for radicals to use to overturn the "establishment." One of the first things you need to understand about Mr. Alinsky and his book, is that he partially dedicated it to Satan. The *Personal Acknowledgments* page says:

> ...*the first radical known to man who rebelled against the establishment and did it so effectively that he at least won his own kingdom—Lucifer.*[154]

In order to not get suckered into this rabbit hole, let's just overlook the fact that Mrs. Clinton and President Obama openly support a man who directly honored Lucifer himself. And you may have noticed the number of rules created by Mr. Alinsky, thirteen. There's that number again. Whether you believe in superstitions or not, one thing you cannot argue is that Mr. Alinsky's *Rules for Radicals* has been very effective for the Left. I won't cover all the radical rules, but let's look at a few.

First, take a moment to think back to the name-calling in the paragraph from EJROC's *Organizing Handbook*. They used phrases such as *angry white parents, misinformation campaign, and TRUMP (gasp!!!)*. Now consider Mr. Alinsky's fifth rule for radicals which says:

[153] Ambinder, M. (2009) *The rise of the Alinsky explanantion, The Atlantic.* Available at: https://www.theatlantic.com/politics/archive/2009/08/the-rise-of-the-alinsky-explanantion/23168/

[154] Alinsky, S. (1971) *Rules for Radicals: A Practical Primer for Realistic Radicals, Full text of 'Rules for radicals'.* Available at: https://archive.org/stream/RulesForRadicals/RulesForRadicals_djvu.txt

> *Ridicule is man's most potent weapon. It is almost impossible to*
> *counterattack ridicule. Also it infuriates the opposition, who then*
> *react to your advantage.*

If you're openly Conservative, how many times have you been called a racist or been ridiculed by your Leftist friends? For me, the number is far too many to count. In fact, the Left has so effectively ridiculed the Right on the topic of racism, it's assumed by many that Conservatism equals racism. Of course, the truth is exactly the opposite.

To understand the effectiveness of ridicule, let's conduct a brief review of racism in America. This is rather long and I apologize for that, but it's important to give you the complete story. First, the Republican Party ended slavery and slave-owners were largely southern Democrats. Accordingly, the Civil War was mainly a fight between northern Republicans and southern Democrats.[155] You'd be surprised by the number of people who don't know this. In fact, African Americans voted Republican for decades before being seduced over to the other side. It was the Democrat Party who enforced 100 years of Jim Crow laws established to intimidate African Americans.[156] Additionally, Democrats founded the Klu Klux Klan to violently terrorize African Americans and Republicans trying to win elections in the South.[157]

According to NPR, African Americans began moving to the Democrat Party during the Depression and the New Deal despite Jim Crow laws

---

[155]Shisler, W.D. (2017) *The history of the Democratic Party and the KKK, Southern Maryland News.* Available at: https://www.somdnews.com/independent/opinion/letters_to_the_editor/the-history-of-the-democratic-party-and-the-kkk/article_802a75c4-34f3-5dcb-8c1a-04a4222c077a.html

[156]Jacobs, S. (2020) *Democrats & Jim Crow: A century of racist history the Democratic Party prefers you'd forget, The Libertarian Institute.* Available at: https://libertarianinstitute.org/articles/democrats-jim-crow-a-century-of-racist-history-the-democratic-party-prefers-youd-forget/

[157]*Grant, reconstruction and the KKK, Public Broadcasting Service.* Available at: https://www.pbs.org/wgbh/americanexperience/features/grant-kkk/

still being strongly enforced in many southern states. The New Deal saw the federal government launch a number of programs to fight the extreme poverty of the time, but it was The Civil Rights Act of 1964 which drove African American support for the Democrats up to 90% or better.[158]

The Civil Rights Act made racial discrimination illegal and somehow the Democrat Party received most of the credit despite strong Republican support and determined Democrat opposition. In the Senate, Republicans voted 82% in favor and Democrats accounted for 78% of the no votes. In the House, Republicans voted 80% in favor and Democrats made up 74% of no votes.[159] In fact, Democrats conducted an infamous 75-day filibuster that almost derailed the Civil Rights act. This remains to this day the longest lasting filibuster in U.S. history.[160]

Also, Democrat President Lyndon Johnson, who signed the Civil Rights Act into law, was notoriously racist and fond of using racial epithets in public conversations. Even dishonest "fact-checkers" like *Snopes* are forced to admit President Johnson used the "N" word constantly while serving in elected office.[161]

In fact, according to MSNBC, a staunch defender of all Leftist causes, President Johnson often referred to any bill supporting minority civil rights as a "n****r bill." MSNBC continues by saying even when appointing the Supreme Court's first African American justice, Thurgood Marshall,

[158] Bates, K.G. (2014) *Why did black voters flee the Republican Party in the 1960s?*, National Public Radio. Available at: https://www.npr.org/sections/codeswitch/2014/07/14/331298996/why-did-black-voters-flee-the-republican-party-in-the-1960s

[159] *Democrat/GOP vote tally on 1964 Civil Rights Act* (2002) *Wall St. Journal*. Available at: https://www.wsj.com/articles/SB1041302509432817073

[160] Riley, R. (2020) *Fact check: Southern Dems held up 1964 Civil Rights Act, set filibuster record at 60 days*, USA Today. Available at: https://www.usatoday.com/story/news/factcheck/2020/06/23/fact-check-democrats-hold-senate-filibuster-record-75-days-1964/3228935001/

[161] Emery, D. (2016) *Did LBJ say 'I'll have those n*****s voting Democratic for 200 years'?*, Snopes. Available at: https://www.snopes.com/fact-check/lbj-voting-democratic/

President Johnson was quoted as saying, "when I appoint a n****r to the bench, I want everybody to know he's a n****r." The MSNBC article also tells the story of President Johnson's African American chauffer who wanted to be called by his name and not "boy" or "n****r." To that request, President Johnson replied:

> As long as you are black, and you're gonna be black till the day you die, no one's gonna call you by your goddamn name. So no matter what you are called, nigger, you just let it roll off your back like water, and you'll make it. Just pretend you're a goddamn piece of furniture.[162]

Many of my Liberal friends like to argue that these events occurred so long ago, they're no longer valid to today's Democrat Party. Really? One of the leaders of that filibuster was Democrat West Virginia Senator Robert Byrd who also happened to be an Exalted Cyclops and well-known recruiter for the KKK.[163] After his death, Hillary Clinton referred to him as her "friend and mentor."[164] Among those who eulogized Senator Byrd at his funeral were President Bill Clinton, President Barack Obama, and President Joe Biden.[165] Arguably, the four most powerful Democrat politi-

---

[162] Serwer, A. (2014) *Lyndon Johnson was a civil rights hero. but also a racist: Lyndon Johnson was a racist. He was also the greatest champion of racial equality to occupy the White House since Lincoln.*, MSNBC. Available at: https://www.msnbc.com/msnbc/lyndon-johnson-civil-rights-racism-msna305591

[163] Headlee, C. (2010) *Did Robert Byrd really change his mind on race?*, WNYC Studios: The Takeaway. Available at: https://www.wnycstudios.org/podcasts/takeaway/articles/69395-did-robert-byrd-really-change-his-mind-race

[164] Dulis, E. (2016) *Flashback: Hillary Clinton praises 'friend and mentor' Robert Byrd (a KKK recruiter)*, Breitbart. Available at: https://www.breitbart.com/politics/2016/08/25/hillary-clinton-friend-mentor-robert-byrd-kkk/

[165] Reuters (2020) *Fact check: Robert Byrd, eulogized by Joe Biden at funeral, was not KKK Grand Wizard*, reuters.com. Available at: https://www.reuters.com/article/idUSKBN26S2E4/

cians of the last three decades were more than happy to overlook Senator Byrd's KKK membership. Democrat racism seems to be alive and well right now.

Returning to The Civil Rights Act of 1964, despite overwhelming Republican support and historically resolute Democrat resistance, Leftists and their willing accomplices in the press successfully framed opposition to the Act on Republican Barry Goldwater. This was seen by African Americans as opposition to civil rights in general. After that, tying racism to the Republican party and ridiculing them in the eyes of people of color was easy. How effective was this ridicule? During my lifetime, I don't remember any Republican Presidential candidate NOT being called a racist going all the way back to President Ronald Reagan.

When President Donald Trump entered the picture, the racism ridicule went into overdrive. The *New York Times* published stories with titles such as, *How Racist is Trump's Republican Party?*"[166] From NPR, we saw headlines like, *From Mom Jokes to Trump-era Racism, Cristela Alonzo Aims to Skewer Latino Stereotypes.*[167] Even before President Trump declared himself a candidate for the 2024 election, the racism ridicule never slowed down. *Salon* published an article in 2022 titled, *Trump Unleashed the Poison of Racism—and New Research Suggests it Will Linger for Years.*[168]

There were also claims President Trump's "racism" showed itself in events like Charlottesville, VA where he allegedly referred to neo-Nazis

---

[166]Thomas (2020) How racist is Trump's Republican Party?, The New York Times. Available at: https://www.nytimes.com/2020/03/18/opinion/trump-republicans-racism.html

[167]Garcia-Navarro, L. (2017) From mom jokes to trump-era racism, Cristela Alonzo aims to skewer Latino stereotypes, NPR. Available at: https://www.npr.org/2017/03/05/518212330/from-mom-jokes-to-trump-era-racism-cristela-alonzo-aims-to-skewer-latino-stereot

[168]DeVega, C. (2022) Trump unleashed the poison of racism—and new research suggests it will linger for years, Salon. Available at: https://www.salon.com/2022/03/03/unleashed-the-poison-of—and-new-research-suggests-it-will-linger-for-years/

as "very fine people." The press stood by this claim for at least two years.[169] The "very fine people" comment occurred three days after the worst of the Charlottesville violence. President Trump's transcript from that day proves these claims are absolutely false.[170] If that's true, how did the press run with the story for so long? Simple. They fabricated a hoax. Unfortunately, it's incredibly easy to do.

To review the events at Charlottesville, the city was planning to remove a statue of Robert E. Lee and remove his name from a nearby park. Two protest groups showed up that day. One supporting the changes and the other opposing them. According to President Trump's transcript from Trump Tower on August 15, 2017, both groups were mostly average citizens using their First Amendment right of peaceful protest, but both were also infiltrated by extremist elements.[171]

The press were outraged when President Trump suggested the alt-Left shared blame for the initial violence. However, the very next day, eyewitness reports in *Slate* magazine confirmed *Antifa* was present in the Leftist group.[172] When neo-Nazis and *Antifa* occupy the same space, there can only be one result. Violence soon followed. After some brief skirmishes, White Nationalist James Alex Fields, Jr. drove his car into a crowd killing Heather Heyer and injuring dozens more.

---

[169] Steadman, O. (2019) *Trump defended the Charlottesville white supremacists—again,* BuzzFeed News. Available at: https://www.buzzfeednews.com/article/otilliasteadman/ trump-charlottesville-defend-white-supremacists

[170] *Read the complete transcript of president Trump's remarks at Trump Tower on Charlottesville* (2017) Los Angeles Times. Available at: https://www.latimes.com/politics/ la-na-pol-trump-charlottesville-transcript-20170815-story.html

[171] *Read the complete transcript of president Trump's remarks at Trump Tower on Charlottesville* (2017) Los Angeles Times. Available at: https://www.latimes.com/politics/ la-na-pol-trump-charlottesville-transcript-20170815-story.html

[172] Lithwick, D. (2017) *What the 'alt-left' trump despises was actually doing in Charlottesville last weekend,* Slate Magazine. Available at: https://slate.com/news-and-politics/2017/08/what-the-alt-left-was-actually-doing-in-charlottesville.html

To understand how the "very fine people" hoax happened, let's first look at President Trump's comments from the day Ms. Heyer was murdered. On August 12th, President Trump said:

> We condemn in the strongest possible terms this egregious display
> of hatred, bigotry and violence on many sides, on many sides. It's
> been going on for a long time in our country...the hate and the divi-
> sion must stop, and must stop right now. We have to come together
> as Americans with love for our nation and true affection— really,
> I say this so strongly, true affection for each other.[173]

For "journalists," these words didn't condemn the White supremacists in strong enough terms and most news stories never mentioned *Antifa* was involved in the violence. Next, on August 14th, President Trump made the following comments from the White House:

> To anyone who acted criminally in this weekend's racist violence,
> you will be held fully accountable. Justice will be delivered. As I
> said on Saturday, we condemn in the strongest possible terms this
> egregious display of hatred, bigotry and violence – it has no place
> in America.[174]

Real Clear Politics was one of the few news outlets to counter the "very fine people" hoax and I reference their story from here to document the

---

[173] Sitrin, C. (2017) *Read: President Trump's remarks condemning violence 'on many sides'* in *Charlottesville*, Vox. Available at: https://www.vox.com/2017/8/12/16138906/ president-trump-remarks-condemning-violence-on-many-sides-charlottesville-rally

[174] *Full text: Trump's statement on white supremacists in Charlottesville* (2017) *POLITICO.* Available at: https://www.politico.com/story/2017/08/14/ full-text-trump-comments-white-supremacists-charlottesville-va-transcript-241618

events. On August 15th, President Trump spoke from Trump Tower to further clarify his comments about neo-Nazis:[175]

> *Excuse me, they didn't put themselves down as neo-Nazis, and you had some very bad people in that group. But you also had people that were very fine people on both sides. You had people in that group — excuse me, excuse me, I saw the same pictures you did. You had people in that group that were there to protest the taking down of, to them, a very, very important statue and the renaming of a park from Robert E. Lee to another name.*

President Trump then more clearly defined "very fine people" when he said:

> *I'm not talking about the neo-Nazis and white nationalists because they should be condemned totally.*

By then, the press smelled blood in the water and the hoax was on. The *Real Clear Politics* story continues by saying:

> *Nonetheless, countless so-called journalists have furthered this damnable lie. For example, MSNBC's Nicolle Wallace responded that Trump had "given safe harbor to Nazis, to white suprema-cists." Her NBC colleague Chuck Todd claimed Trump "gave me the wrong kind of chills. Honestly, I'm a bit shaken from what I just heard."*

---

[175] Cortes, S. (2019) *Trump didn't call Neo-Nazis 'fine people.' here's proof., Real Clear Politics.* Available at: https://www.realclearpolitics.com/articles/2019/03/21/trump_didnt_call_neo-nazis_fine_people_heres_proof_139815.html

Later on August 15ᵗʰ from the White House, President Trump tried to clarify his comments one more time:

> *Racism is evil, and those who cause violence in its name are crim-*
> *inals and thugs, including the KKK, neo-Nazis, white suprema-*
> *cists, and other hate groups that are repugnant to everything we*
> *hold dear as Americans.*

Despite these very clear comments, for years afterwards, the press continued to say President Trump called the neo-Nazis at Charlottesville "very fine people"[176] and continued to make claims such as *he still hasn't condemned racism.*[177] The relentless ridicule of President Trump was very effective. Even today, if you talk to many people of color about President Trump, many still assume he's racist and overlook the positive gains made by people of color resulting from his programs.

For example, under President Trump's policies, people of color made historic economic gains. The U.S. Department of Labor showed 5.2 million new jobs created from 2017 to 2019. An amazing 86% of those new hires were people of color. Despite this uplifting news, 12% of African American men and 6% of African American women voted for President Trump in the 2020 election. If you can believe it, both numbers are historically high for Republicans during the last 50 years.[178]

The effectiveness of ridicule cannot be overstated. Just the allegation of racism throws people off their game. As Mr. Alinsky said, *It is almost*

---

[176] Coaston, J. (2019) *Trump's new defense of his Charlottesville comments is incredibly false,* Vox. Available at: https://www.vox.com/2019/4/26/18517980/ trump-unite-the-right-racism-defense-charlottesville

[177] O'Brien, T.L. (2018) *Trump still fails to condemn racism a year after Charlottesville,* Bloomberg.com. Available at: https://www.bloomberg.com/view/articles/2018-08-12/ trump-still-fails-to-condemn-racism-a-year-after-charlottesville

[178] Collins, S. (2020) *Trump made gains with black voters in some states. here's why.,* Vox. Available at: https://www.vox.com/2020/11/4/21537966/trump-black-voters-exit-polls

impossible to counterattack ridicule. They don't need to prove you're a racist, they just need to accuse you of racism. Now, you're forced to prove you're not racist. Once that happens, they've already won, and your reaction is their advantage. Sixty years after Mr. Alinsky's death, Republicans and Conservatives must still constantly prove they aren't racist. Yes, ridicule is VERY effective.

Next, the eighth rule for radicals says:

> *Keep the pressure on, with different tactics and actions, and utilize all events of the period for your purpose.*

Again, if we revisit the that same paragraph of EJROC's *Organizing Handbook*, they certainly employed radicals' eighth rule. Consider the following sentences. *Schools that don't teach CRT want to cover up systemic racism and …droves of angry white parents are getting mobilized for the midterm elections to take back Congress.* This next one is a doozy. *Their efforts has been conceived by former Trump strategists, funded by billionaire donors throwing tens of millions of dollars at the misinformation campaign, and managed by some of the same right-wing organizations driving racist voter suppression laws across the country.*

I composed a list of ridicule statements from these three sentences. They are CRT opponents are racist, they want to lie about history, you should hate White parents who vote, you should hate Trump and his former employees, you should hate rich people and their misinformation campaigns, and finally, you should hate Voter ID laws. That's a pretty thorough list touching upon several topics that have nothing to do with CRT, but everything to do with the other hot topics of our time. EJROC certainly *utilized all events of the period for their purpose.*

Next, the ninth rule for radicals says:

> *The threat is usually more terrifying than the thing itself.*

An example of the threat being more terrifying than "the thing itself" occurred to me on social media when people called me racist for sharing my conservative ideas. At first, I must admit it was difficult. They ganged up on me and repeatedly attacked me for every single post. For a while, even my most neutral comments generated nasty replies.

However, as time passed, I began to realize these attacks changed nothing in my life. My true friends were still my true friends. Of course, a few people who only knew me casually began to look at me differently, but what was the genuine impact? The answer was very little.

Not to plead completely innocent, I soon learned to use these attacks to my advantage. I stole an Alinsky rule by adding ridicule and sarcasm into my posts. I certainly incited Leftists to attack me and it drove them out of their minds. It was very entertaining and I soon began enjoying their rabid responses more than I should have. I began receiving threats such as, "I'm going to unfriend you! I'm gonna do it! I really am!" My usual response was, "Ciao, baby! Have a good life. Take care."

As if unfriending me was going to somehow hurt my feelings. Something I considered many times during this period, What Would Jesus Do? Certainly not what I was doing. That's for sure and we definitely know He didn't approve of my fun, but He forgave me anyway. Thankfully.

Despite my bad behavior, a positive outcome soon emerged. Some people outed themselves toward me and I learned their true nature. People who I believed were my true friends, showed me they were not. For that, I will always be grateful. Frankly, looking back, their friendship was never worth my time. Eventually, as they saw their attacks were pointless, they began to give up.

At one point, I had several people who attacked me daily on social media and I suspect a few may have been working together. Now, I have one or two who only bother with me once a month or so and my true friends are still my true friends. As Mr. Alinsky said, the threats were worse than the thing and the thing itself had no teeth.

Let's do one more rule. The seventh radical rule says:

> *A tactic that drags on too long becomes a drag. Man can sustain militant interest in any issue for only a limited time, after which it becomes a ritualistic commitment, like going to church on Sunday mornings.*

This is one rule Leftists have seemingly overlooked. Calling everyone and everything "racist" all the time has certainly become a drag. It seems most people are getting fed up with the name calling from the Left. FINALLY. I could not be happier and, if you've read this far into the book, I'm sure you agree.

Winning Racial Justice in Our Schools: Resisting the Right-Wing Attacks on Critical Race Theory Organizing Toolkit (OTK)

Now that we have a basic understanding of *Rules for Radicals*, let's dig back into the OTK. There we will find the tactics you will likely face when confronting CRT supporters. One tactic is telling the opposite of the truth. Yes, this is also called lying, but it's a specific kind of lie.

In this lie, if you're doing something wrong, accuse your opponent of doing that same thing to deflect attention away from your own bad actions. Many attribute this to Saul Alinsky from *Rules for Radicals*, but I was unable to find it there. I'm not saying Mr. Alinsky didn't create that tactic. I'm just saying I didn't find that particular quote or strategy in my copy of *Rules for Radicals*, where it is popularly sourced. However, the OTK shows that tactic is alive and well as a Leftist strategy.

Defining the Opposition (that's you and me)

Not surprisingly, the OTK opens by defining CRT opponents as racists who want to hide the truth about real history and avoid confronting systemic racism in our schools. Again, let's return to that paragraph in the OTK that we've already discussed a few times:

> ...*the Right is amping up their racist strategies – and their newest tactic is attacking critical race theory (CRT)...most importantly for the Right, droves of angry white parents are getting mobilized for the midterm elections to take back Congress.*

After reading this sentence several times now, in your opinion, which side seems determined to employ racist strategies? Which side has groups such as BLM and Antifa mobilizing and using violence to achieve their political goals? Granted, plenty of parents have become angry, but why? As we documented in Chapter One, Leftists are lying to them about their children's education. That's enough to get parents of all races riled up.

Counter-Narrating the Attacks on Critical Race Theory

One funny thing about the OTK is that it's full of CRT. For example, the OTK links to a document, titled *Guide: Counter-Narrating the Attacks on Critical Race Theory*[179] (even though it doesn't exist). If you remember, counter-narrating or counter-storytelling is a primary CRT principle which can include all, some, or none of the truth. Plus, this document has CRT right in the title.

In Liberal La-La Land where every parent is a neo-Nazi, Leftists imagine parents complaining about CRT and the things they might say to "breed racial resentment." Of course, it's the Leftists who actually breed racial resentment. Here are some of those imagined comments from the Guide. They're followed by my commentary which exposes how they

---

[179] *Guide: Counter-narrating the attacks on critical race theory* (2021) *Race Forward.* Available at: https://www.raceforward.org/sites/default/files/Guide%20to%20Counter-Narrating%20the%20Attacks%20on%20Critical%20Race%20Theory%20-%20Race%20Forward_2021-06-14.pdf

use slight half-truths in their tactics. Remember, these statements are IMAGINED comments coming from parents who oppose CRT:

> **Imagined Parental Comment:** *Talking about race is inherently "divisive."*

My Commentary: No, talking about race the way THEY want to talk about race is inherently divisive. It's very possible to talk about race without dividing students into different oppressor and oppressed groups.

> **Imagined Parental Comment:** *Systemic racism is not real.*

My Commentary: Systemic racism is real, but it's the Left who support it with programs like *Affirmative Action*. Keep in mind, as part of systemic racism, Leftists like to say school curricula are designed to make students of color fail. Personally, I don't think our educators are smart enough to create textbooks that makes White students succeed and oppress minority students at the same time.

> **Imagined Parental Comment:** *White people will be "victims" when we talk about race or address systemic racism in any meaningful way.*

My Commentary: White people will only be victims when talking about race when teachers purposefully make White students victims when talking about race. Again, it's very possible to talk about race without dividing students into different oppressor and oppressed groups.

The supposedly racist narratives are then followed with this paragraph:

> *We know these narratives, while false, are highly effective because all of us have been socialized in a dominant culture that reinforces*

these narratives. Counteracting their narrative attack with telling the facts about critical race theory will, therefore, not be as effective as we would want it to be.

Translation: Just telling the truth isn't enough to defeat parents who oppose CRT. Leftists claim they're forced to create talking points because the Right are masters of talking points and propaganda. According to the OTK, they're just trying to keep up.

I'm not sure if you've noticed while reading this book, but Leftists are the Mac Daddy's of talking points and propaganda. For an example, let's review our earlier discussion about Officer Darren Wilson's justified shooting of Michael Brown. False witness accounts said Mr. Brown had his hands raised in surrender and begged for his life at the time of the shooting. This was later proven false, but the scenario played perfectly into the Leftist narrative of a racist America.[180]

"Hands up, don't shoot" became a rally cry across the nation. We even saw several lawmakers use the slogan before speaking at the U.S. House of Representatives. After it was proven false, the Left continued to use the slogan. For example, six months after the evidence came out, NPR still reported "hands up, don't shoot" endures.[181] The story even quotes then-Attorney General Eric Holder who said:

> *It remains not only valid but essential to question how such a strong alternative version of events was able to take hold so swiftly and to be accepted so readily.*

---

[180]Capeheart, J. (2015) *'Hands up, don't shoot' was built on a lie, The Washington Post.* Available at: https://www.washingtonpost.com/blogs/post-partisan/wp/2015/03/16/lesson-learned-from-the-shooting-of-michael-brown/

[181]Corley, C. (2015) *Whether history or hype, 'hands up, don't shoot' endures,* NPR. Available at: https://www.npr.org/2015/08/08/430411141/whether-history-or-hype-hands-up-dont-shoot-endures

Translation: the whole world was wrong about Michael Brown, but everyone believed it because, in our racist nation, White cops shooting unarmed Black people in the streets is a daily occurrence. You may even believe this yourself. Of course, the facts say differently.

For example, in 2019, researchers from Michigan State University and the University of Maryland compiled statistics from 900 fatal U.S. police shootings from 2015. Researchers found *no racial bias* among the police shootings. In fact, they found officers were most likely to shoot civilians of their own race. This was true for African American, White, and Hispanic American officers.[182] Around the same time this research was published, five full years after Michael Brown, during the Democratic presidential debate, eight candidates still talked about Mr. Brown as an unarmed Black teenager murdered by a White cop. The candidates also repeatedly used sayings such as our nation needed to take a good hard look at itself concerning race relations.[183]

Why were these Democrat politicians so determined to continue taking advantage of Mr. Brown's death after 'hands up, don't shoot" was proven false years earlier? A quote from Rahm Emanuel, former Obama White House Chief of Staff, offers one possible reason:

You never let a serious crisis go to waste. And what I mean by that it's an opportunity to do things you think you could not do before.[184]

Rahm Emanuel
Former Obama White House Chief of Staff, 2009-10

---

[182] Bawagan, J. (2019) *Study that claims white police no more likely to shoot minorities draws fire*, Science. Available at: https://www.science.org/content/article/study-claims-white-police-no-more-likely-shoot-minorities-draws-fire

[183] Attkisson, S. (2019) *Time to retire Ferguson Narrative*, The Hill. Available at: https://thehill.com/opinion/civil-rights/457049-time-to-retire-ferguson-narrative/

[184] *Rahm Emanuel–you never let a serious crisis go to waste...*, Brainy Quote. Available at: https://www.brainyquote.com/quotes/rahm_emanuel_409199

According to these sentiments by Mr. Emanuel, Democrats continued to use "Hands up, don't shoot" because they could still get mileage from it. To further explain, first, they gain a political advantage by making America seem as racist as possible. All Republicans and conservatives are racist, right? Next, "Hands up, don't shoot," was all over the news for weeks and months. When proven false, the press reported it, but not nearly with the vigor and wall-to-wall coverage of the original story. EVERYONE saw the original Michael Brown stories in the press. Limited numbers of Americans saw the retractions.

Centrally Controlled Talking Points

In order to keep pro-CRT social justice warriors using approved messaging, the OTK includes pre-written, centrally-controlled talking points to counter the "racist" talking points of the Right. Afterall, Leftists are just trying to keep up. If you remember Mr. Limbaugh's and Mr. Larsen's seminar callers, they pretended to be grassroots citizens concerned about a cause, but in reality, they were organized community activists.

This is an example of Leftists organizing volunteers and/or paid employees while accusing Right wing groups of doing the same. *When you're doing something, accuse your opposition of that same thing.* And yes, with just a little basic research, I found Left wing groups seem to be much better organized than Right wing groups. One example, the Talk Radio Initiative came straight from the DNC and the Clinton White House. Mr. Limbaugh and Mr. Larsen had only themselves and their small teams of employees to fight back.

Another example, going back to Chapter One and the Riverside Unified School District (RUSD), in the school board meetings, the speakers supporting CRT (even though it doesn't exist) were almost exclusively representing local activist groups. Other supporters were teachers representing groups such as the local teachers' union. Keep in mind, teachers' unions aren't supposed to be activist groups, but often behave like them. I do give all of these representatives credit for one thing, however. Unlike the participants in the Talk Radio Initiative, all RUSD activists clearly identified themselves.

In these school board meetings, pro-CRT speakers often sounded like they were reading professionally pre-prepared talking points which all sounded very similar to each other. In the YouTube video of that RUSD meeting, the self-identified pro-CRT activists each delivered sentences which sounded polished and focus grouped.

To further explain, many advocacy organizations use focus groups to test and polish talking points and branding statements. In these meetings, they throw out various ideas to a group of well-paid, like-minded activists. The ones that resonate are kept and used later at events such as School Board meetings. The others are tossed out.

At the RUSD school board meeting, in just a seven-minute time span during a two-hour meeting, four pro-CRT activists used four polished talking points while speaking.[185] If you choose to use the hyperlink provided below to watch the video, and I encourage you to do so, I've included the timecodes for each comment.

During those seven minutes, first, we heard (at approximately 54:00) the importance of being taught history *by someone that looks like you.* Second, (at approximately 56:30) forcing students to learn a curriculum into which *they do not fit.* Third, (at approximately 58:18) *this is the time... we must seize the moment.* And, fourth, (at approximately 01:01:00) *diversity makes us smarter.* Keep in mind, these talking points were most likely not written in Riverside County, California. CRT supporters across the country repeatedly use all four of these statements, especially the one that says it's important to be taught by *someone that looks like you.*

CRT supporters who made these comments tended to represent organizations such as the *BLU Educational Foundation, AntiRacist Riverside, the*

[185] *Live stream: RUSD board meeting 9-15-2020* (2020) *YouTube.* Available at: https://www.youtube.com/watch?v=MI1AJ7AhC7I

National Association for the Advancement of Colored People (NAACP), *Stand Up Riverside, Center Against Racism & Trauma,* etc. All organizations which openly support CRT and their representatives often attend several meetings in different school districts to support their various agendas.

One *BLU Educational Foundation* representative even said she was glad to be in, "Rialto" when she meant to say, "Riverside" during her remarks in the RUSD meeting. Rialto is a southern California town near Riverside. She quickly corrected herself and moved on, but it was obvious she was reading from a script that she was using at several different School Board meetings. Just to be sure, I emailed her and asked if she attends different school meetings in the area. She said, "Yes." She was one of the few who had the courage to respond to my email inquiries while writing this book and I appreciate her honest response.

On the flip side, the anti-CRT speakers were identified exclusively as parents. If you watch the video, starting at the 03:15:00 mark (yes, that's two full hours after the activists were given their time to speak), parents shared their concerns about CRT with the RUSD school board. They also read from scripts, but they were obviously not polished nor professionally written. They also didn't include very similar, and possibly coordinated, catch phrases or talking points. The parent's portion of the video runs about seven minutes in duration and includes an RUSD board member making a snotty retort to claims that RUSD teaches CRT. I highly encourage you to watch it. It's very entertaining.[186]

I do give Leftists credit for one thing. They're very good at this stuff. When reading these expertly crafted talking points, their effect even on an old news veteran like myself, is surprising. For example, when reading the talking point, *CRT opponents want to deny children a real education,* I actually feel shame at first. Like I was doing something wrong by opposing CRT. For just a moment, I ask myself, am I on the wrong side here? Am I

---

[186] *Live stream: RUSD board meeting 9-15-2020* (2020) *YouTube.* Available at: https://www. youtube.com/watch?v=Ml1AJ7AhC7I

really trying to deny children a real education? Then I take a moment and recognize the embedded propaganda and remember, Marxists never provide a real education. *When you're doing something, accuse your opposition of that same thing.*

We've discussed this phenomenon before. I'm an educated adult, knowledgeable on this subject, and I'm still influenced by sneaky half-truths and mispresented facts. Now, think how they impact you and, more importantly, your children. Consider your feelings as you read the upcoming talking points from the OTK. They're skillfully crafted to make you feel guilty for opposing their agenda. In the following list, just like before, I present each professionally prepared talking point following by my commentary. They read:

> **Polished Talking Point:** *Children deserve an honest education about race and racism in this country. Attempts to squash these conversations are attacks on a multiracial democracy, justice, and community.*

My commentary: Of course, the sneaky misrepresentation here is that the only honest conversation about racism is *their* relentlessly negative version which says America is permanently racist and stuck in 1955 Alabama. Anything different is a dishonest, racist attack on justice, democracy, and your local community.

> **Polished Talking Point:** *Critical race theory asserts that it is essential to incorporate voices and stories that have historically been excluded from schools. Learning true history helps youth understand the world they are living in, and answer the questions they have about that world.*

My commentary: The sneaky misrepresentation here is that the history taught in schools today is the exact same history taught 100 years ago when 90% of the U.S. population was White.[187] In reality, removing CRT from schools does not mean ignoring the histories of all people of color. Remember, CRT and Ethnic Studies are not the same thing. You can teach one group about their history without shaming others.

> *Polished Talking Point: We cannot allow public officials to dumb down public school curricula because they are not comfortable with the truth of this country's past and present.*

My commentary: The sneaky misrepresentation here is that removing CRT from school curricula means dumbing down the quality of public education. On the contrary, if we want to dumb down public schools, we should keep CRT in schools and bully students with it. Furthermore, people who oppose CRT are not racist cowards afraid to face the real history of our nation. They want to protect their children from CRT's *Psychology of Shame.* By now, as mentioned before, I hope you're beginning to recognize their tactics and strategies.

Media Kit

The OTK also links to a Media Kit to teach social justice warriors how to talk to the press. This includes pre-prepared talking points, of course. Created by the *African American Policy Forum, Black Lives Matter at School,* and the *Zinn Education Project,* you probably already realize the kit is a Leftist playbook for manipulating the press. Titled *Media Training 101: General Tips & Preparation,* the kit says when it comes to talking points, *"don't think you need to make up your own; repetition and echoing of messages is good."*

---

[187] *United States Census: 1920* (1920) *United States Census.* Available at: https://www2.census.gov/library/publications/decennial/1920/volume-3/41084484v3ch01.pdf

The media training kit tells activists to "*do your homework.*" Prepare for questions such as *What is CRT?*, *Is CRT dividing us?*, and *Is CRT taught in K-12 schools?* While researching this book, I heard these exact same questions more times than I can count. Again, they are very well organized.

Remember Secretary of Education Cardona's appearance on *The View?* To refresh your memory, one show host asked Dr. Cardona, "*Is Critical Race Theory, as it's being bandied about right now, taught in K through 12?*" I don't know if *The View* host used this exact same media kit, but her questions and comments sounded exactly like the media prep provided in this package. Of course, Dr. Cardona denied CRT in schools before a national audience, but, as we have learned, the evidence says otherwise.

The kit also instructs protestors to consider the final format of their interview. Typical television news stories are shorter than two minutes. To help the "journalist" push CRT (and they do push CRT), activists are told to give clear and concise soundbites. In journalism, soundbites are the same thing as talking points. When soundbites are clear and concise, they're effective and easy to edit into a story. An example of a good soundbite is, *children deserve an honest education about race and racism in this country.* This soundbite features brevity. It's less than five seconds long and it portrays CRT opponents as deceptive liars and racists who want to hide the truth. Definitely professionally written and polished.

The media kit offers a number of soundbites for CRT supporters to memorize and regurgitate to "journalists." The questions almost don't even matter. If the "journalist" asks an off-topic question, the media kit suggests using their pre-prepared talking points to bring the interview back on-subject. The next time you see an interview, watch for this technique. You'll soon notice people being interviewed often don't answer the questions they were just asked. Instead, they just repeat one of their talking points. Happens all the time. Now, let's take a look at some of the talking points for the press included in the toolkit. Just like before, each is followed with my commentary:

> *Polished Talking Point: Teaching about systemic racism and sexism provides a bridge to unite us.*

My commentary: The sneaky misrepresentation here is that creating conflict among students of different races and sexes brings everyone together. No, it doesn't. CRT is designed to divide and shame students. Make no mistake. The media kit authors completely understand this. If you remember back to the chapter about the North Carolina Task Force, CRT lesson plans often include *White Shaming* and *Male Shaming*.

Now let's take a deeper look at CRT shaming tactics. In 2022, social media influencer *Libs of TikTok* posted a CRT lesson plan for kindergarteners sent to her by a parent.[188] Incredibly, the lesson plan was about *Freedom* and the 5-year-old children were instructed to explore the following phrases:

> *Black people have less and white have more [sic].*
> *Whites make it harder for black people.*
> *Whites boss around POC (People of Color).*
> *Threatening body language.*
> *You have to fight in a war.*

Does that sound like bridge-building to you? Do those statements appear as if they would facilitate a discussion about freedom? To me, this looks like another example of the *Psychology of Shame* discovered by *Moms For Liberty* in *Wit & Wisdom.* How will African American children view White children after this lesson? How will White children view themselves? CRT teaches hate and division, plain and simple.

One repeated trend from pro-CRT educators is grammatical errors in lesson plans. These are the people teaching your children to read and write. You may have noticed one phrase in the lesson plan said, *Black people have*

---

[188] *Kindergarteners taught 'whites make it harder for black people'* (2022) *Libs of TikTok.* Available at: https://www.libsoftiktok.com/p/kindergarteners-taught-whites-make

less and white have more [sic]. I think this professional teacher and CRT advocate meant to say "Whites" have more.

> **Polished Talking Point:** *This well-funded and coordinated disinformation campaign is brought to you by conservative think tanks that have for decades sought to undermine public education.*

My commentary: The sneaky misrepresentation here is that CRT opponents are not concerned parents who formed grassroots organizations to fight back against CRT. They want you to believe CRT opponents are under-handed Conservatives who use dishonest arguments to keep your children stupid and they are well-funded by obviously racist billionaires. This brings us back, one more time, to a Saul Alinsky-type tactic often used by Leftists. *When you're doing something, accuse your opposition of that same thing.* In reality, it's actually Marxists who need a dumbed down population to achieve their political goals. Also, if you think back to BLM's list of corporate donors, CRT supporters are the ones most likely funded by obviously racist billionaires.

The next media kit talking point explores a "dumbed down" education further:

> **Polished Talking Point:** *We cannot allow politicians to dumb down public education to satisfy their narrow definition of "patriotic education."*

My commentary: Again, the sneaky misrepresentation here is that removing CRT from school curricula means dumbing down your child's education. We've seen the code words "dumb down" used several times now. You can be sure the phrase was brainstormed, professionally polished, and focus grouped to ensure its effectiveness. Also, its use in more than one talking point reinforces the strategy that repetition and echoing of messages is good. This talking point also reveals another common Leftist strategy, trying to define patriotism as racist and narrow-minded.

> **Polished Talking Point:** *A public education that seeks to serve only some of its students is deeply unfair and un-American.*

My commentary: The sneaky misrepresentation here is that removing CRT from school curricula means only serving the needs of White students. Nothing could be further from the truth. Remember, anti-racists say some of the most racist things you've ever heard.

PRIMARY LESSONS: CRT activists project their own traits and actions onto their opponents. *When you're doing something, accuse your opposition of that same thing.* They claim Right wing groups opposing CRT are well-funded and well-organized. When in fact, *they* are well-funded and well-organized. They have the nation's top educators supporting and working for their cause including the Secretary of Education, the largest teacher's union in the country, and the United Nations. Their tactics are time-tested and effective.

The smartest thing you can do here is to steal those tactics. You may notice I mocked CRT supporters all through this book. This is especially evident in this book's audio version. I simply stole an Alinsky tactic, *ridicule is man's most potent weapon*, and used it against them. Don't try to reinvent the wheel. You may not have all the education publishers, teachers' unions, school boards, and press working for you, but you can adopt their strategies. Download, study, and repurpose their OTK, including all linked sources and documents. You can find the hyperlink to their OTK below.[189]

---

[189] *Winning racial justice in our schools: Resisting the right wing attacks on Critical Race Theory* (2021) Education Justice Research and Organizing Collaborative, New York University Steinhardt . Available at: https://static1.squarespace.com/static/5bc5da7c3560c36b7dab1922/t/6126241c56874d431487 6f6a/1629889575567/CRT+Toolkit+FINAL+August+2021.pdf

CHAPTER NINE

CLOSING THE ACHIEVEMENT GAP

Introduction

CRT SUPPORTERS SAY Ethnic Studies programs help students of color by increasing self-awareness and the research supports these claims. Self-understanding is key to releasing your potential and finding your place in this world. Everyone has unique gifts and self-awareness helps you find your distinct talents.

This isn't something the human race just discovered. 1 Peter 4:10 says, "*As each has received a gift, use it to serve one another, as good stewards of God's varied grace.*" In other words, use your God-given talents to help others. What are your God-given talents? For me, that was a question that took many years to answer. Your experiences may be similar unless you were one of the lucky ones who found your path early in life. Unfortunately, many of us can't see the forest because the trees are in our way. Regarding students of color, ethnic studies provides self-awareness benefits and scholastic improvements as well.

Again, research backs up these claims, but the larger question is can ethnic studies help close the achievement gap? We've already discussed this, but, again, it's important to understand ethnic studies and CRT are **not** one and the same. As I said in this book's *Introduction*, you *can* teach students of color about their history without shaming the White students in the same room.

CRT supporters claim their focus on systemic racism and White supremacy creates positive benefits, but parents say their children suffer from depression and anxiety after attending CRT classes. In this case, I'm certainly more likely to believe parents over politically-motivated educators. CRT focuses on the negative and that logically creates negative results for your child. No college degree required to reach that conclusion. On the opposite side, can a positive-focused ethnic studies curriculum create positive results regarding the achievement gap? In my opinion, absolutely.

Stanford Ethnic Studies Research

Many CRT supporters use Stanford's Ethnic Studies Research (SESR) as the justification for CRT mandates (even though CRT doesn't exist). In 2016, SESR studied the impact of race and cultural studies on school attendance and academic performance for at-risk students. SESR found the scholastic performance of these students dramatically improved after taking a year-long ethnic studies class.[190]

The research paper titled, *The Causal Effects of Cultural Relevance: Evidence From an Ethnic Studies Curriculum*, notes the achievement gap for students of color has been *"disturbingly large and stubbornly persistent."* For example, using *National Assessment of Educational Progress* statistics, SESR found the mathematics proficiency of African American and Hispanic American students is two to three years behind White students. Also, students of color are twice as likely to drop out of high school than their White counterparts.[191]

---

[190] Donald, B. (2016) *Stanford study suggests academic benefits to ethnic studies courses: New research shows gains in attendance, GPA of at-risk high school students from incorporating culturally relevant pedagogy*, Stanford News. Available at: https://news.stanford.edu/2016/01/12/ethnic-studies-benefits-011216/

[191] Dee, T. and Penner, E. (2016) *The causal effects cultural relevance: Evidence from an ethnic studies curriculum*, National Bureau of Economic Research. Available at: https://www.nber.

However, there is some good news here as well. According to the U.S. Census Bureau, 90% of all U.S. adults have a high school diploma. For African Americans, that number is 88% which is a marked improvement from the 1940's when they lagged 17% behind the general population. When we look at college educations, the numbers aren't quite as strong, but still show marked improvement for African Americans.

According to U.S. Census Bureau statistics for 2019, for all U.S. adults, aged 55 years or older, 31% have Bachelor's degrees. Meanwhile, for African Americans from the same age group, 20% graduated from four-year colleges. When we consider younger adults from 54 to 25 years old, that's where we see younger African Americans are much more likely to attend college than previous generations. From that age group, 36% of all U.S. adults have Bachelor's degrees. For African Americans, 26% have graduated from four-year schools.[192] Again, the numbers reveal positive news. Among younger adults, African American college graduation rates are growing faster than the U.S. population at large. However, that doesn't mean our work is done. Graduation rates for people of color should continue to improve in the coming years, but if we incorporate positive-centered Ethnic Studies programs, I would like to think we'll see greater gains.

Returning to the Stanford research, SESR uses the term *culturally relevant pedagogy* (CRP) to describe their ethnic studies research. *Culturally relevant pedagogy* is academic-geek-speak for teaching African American cultural history to African American children and Hispanic American cultural history to Hispanic American children. According to the SESR, ethnic studies classes have a positive impact on students of color, so let's start there.

Self-study and self-awareness have great value! Something we've known for centuries. Another long held belief, when you provide at-risk students

---

org/system/files/working_papers/w21865/w21865.pdf

[192]Cheeseman Day, J. (2021) *88% of blacks have a high school diploma, 26% a bachelor's degree, Census.gov.* Available at: https://www.census.gov/library/stories/2020/06/black-high-school-attainment-nearly-on-par-with-national-average.html

with school lessons that interest them, they perform better. Knock me over with a feather. That's the basic theme behind every underdog story ever made. In fact, Dr. Emily Penner, co-author of the Stanford research, says:

> *Schools have tried a number of approaches to support struggling students, and few have been this effective. It's a novel approach that suggests that making school relevant and engaging to struggling students can really pay off.*

Hard to disagree. However, I oppose the SESR researchers' next assertion. They also claim ethnic studies are *more* effective when tied to critical social engagement. You should immediately recognize what that means and I expect nothing less from California Bay Area academic researchers. In other words, ethnic studies classes work best when they also create social justice warriors. I cannot disagree more. In my opinion, in positive ethnic studies programs, we have perhaps the most exciting tool for increasing the scholastic performance of students of color…ever. Unfortunately, Leftists have stolen it for their own purposes.

Let's take a brief look at negative vs. positive thinking. Then, let's consider the potential long-term results of negative ethnic studies vs. positive ethnic studies. Which brings me back to my favorite joke; only an academic would be so stupid as to believe berating White children for being White is a great way to boost the academic performance of students of color.

Negative Thinking

The damaging effects of negative thinking are well established. According to the *National Allegiance on Mental Illness* (NAMI), people with depression are 40% more likely to develop health problems such heart disease and diabetes. Additionally, people with a mental illness are more likely to suffer from substance abuse and unemployment. They're also more likely to drop out of school.[193] NAMI research also says one in six children, ages 6-17, experience a mental health disorder and among youth, ages 10-14, suicide is the 2nd leading cause of death. In addition, three million adolescents, ages 12-17, report serious thoughts of suicide each year.

Healthyplace.com identifies various forms of anxiety as the most common mental illness in the United States for people of all ages.[194] They also say depression and negative thinking often go hand-in-hand. Furthermore, researchers at University College London say they found a connection between repetitive negative thinking and cognitive decline associated with dementia later in life.[195]

Now, let's consider the impact of CRT on a child who may be suffering from anxiety or depression *before* the lesson begins. For example, let's review the phrases in a kindergarten CRT class as reported by one parent on *Libs of TikTok*. The phrases said, *Black people have less and white [sic] have more. Whites make it harder for black people. Whites boss around POC (People of Color). Threatening body language.* And *You have to fight in a war.*

Now consider that child attending similar lessons until high school graduation and how those classes may impact the rest of that child's life. It might mean the difference between successfully managing a mental illness or suffering from one throughout adult life, or worse. Would you expect positive results from the CRT lesson we just reviewed? In my opinion, only a fool or an academic would.

---

[193] *Mental health by the numbers, National Alliance on Mental Illness.* Available at: https://www.nami.org/mhstats

[194] Smith, E.-M. (2022) *Negative thinking and depression: How one fuels the other, HealthyPlace.* Available at: https://www.healthyplace.com/self-help/positivity/negative-thinking-and-depression-how-one-fuels-the-other

[195] Pratt, E. (2020) *Negative thinking can harm your brain and increase your dementia risk, Healthline.* Available at: https://www.healthline.com/health-news/negative-thinking-can-harm-brain-increase-dementia-risk#What-the-study-revealed

Positive Thinking

Fortunately, if your child shows signs of negative thinking associated with CRT, or any other reason, there are things you can do. Setting an example of optimism can make a huge difference. In fact, according to the Mayo Clinic, optimism and pessimism affect many areas of mental and physical well-being. In their article titled, *Positive thinking: Stop negative self-talk to reduce stress,*[196] research shows positive thinking can lead to:

- *Increased life span*
- *Lower rates of depression*
- *Lower levels of distress and pain*
- *Greater resistance to illnesses*
- *Better psychological and physical well-being*
- *Better cardiovascular health and reduced risk of death from cardiovascular disease and stroke*
- *Reduced risk of death from cancer*
- *Reduced risk of death from respiratory conditions*
- *Reduced risk of death from infections*
- *Better coping skills during hardships and times of stress*

If you believe your child engages in negative thinking, the Mayo Clinic offers a few simple considerations. While designed for adults, these considerations certainly have some value when assessing your child. It goes without saying, if you believe your child suffers with a serious mental issue, you should take them to see a doctor immediately so they can receive proper medical attention. For less severe cases, you can consider assessing your child's mental health by asking these questions:

---

[196] *Positive thinking: Stop negative self-talk to reduce stress* (2023) *Mayo Clinic.* Available at: https://www.mayoclinic.org/healthy-lifestyle/stress-management/in-depth/positive-thinking/art-20043950

1. *Does your child focus on the negatives in situations and dismiss the positives?*
2. *When something bad happens, does your child assume it's his/her fault?*
3. *Does your child always assume the worst before knowing the facts?*
4. *Does your child blame others for his/her life challenges?*
5. *Does your child make minor problems into major issues?*
6. *Does your child get anxious about not being perfect?*
7. *Does your child see everything as good or bad with no middle ground?*

After going through this list, if you believe your child may suffer from negative thinking, the Mayo Clinic suggests making a few changes to help them be more positive:

1. **Identify areas to change** – Find one area in your child's life about which they normally complain and identify one thing they like about it. For example, if they complain about taking out the trash, remind them they get rewarded in some way for the task.

2. **Occasionally check on them** – During the day, see how they're doing. If they respond in a negative fashion, try to direct them to something positive. For example, the internet is slow right now, but we can work on that puzzle you like until the internet situation improves.

3. **Be open to humor** – Try to find something that makes them laugh. Engage them in a favorite past time.

4. **Follow a healthy lifestyle** – Try to get them to exercise instead of playing video games all day. Exercise positively affects mood and reduces stress. Also, a healthy diet fuels the mind and body. Finally, make sure they get enough sleep.

5. **Surround them with positive people** – If certain friends and/or family tend to be negative, try to spend more time with positive, supportive people you trust.

6. **Practice positive talk** – As a parent, you have a tremendous influence over your child. Before correcting them for a mistake, consider ways to be gentle and encouraging. For example, you spilled your drink. Clean it up and let's think of ways to prevent it in the future, as opposed to OMG! What did you do? That can be tough sometimes, but with practice, it will become easier. Also, consider talking out loud about the things in your life which make you grateful. For example, I'm glad you're home from school or that shirt looks good on you.

Know & Love: Personality Quiz for Kids

Based on the adult-centered Myers-Briggs personality test (more on Myers-Briggs in the next section), Know & Love (K&L) created a child's self-discovery test. I highly recommend this test for all children and I share it with parents all the time.

K&L designed the test for children to deepen their understanding of themselves and their relationships with others. Again, self-understanding plays a big role in your child's life success and your understanding of your child plays a big role in your success as a parent. An extra bonus, you'll be glad to hear I found no CRT while exploring K&L's website.

The K&L personality test consists of about 30 questions where children select between two different answers. Typical answer selections are *I prefer to play with a few close friends*, or *I prefer to play with lots of friends*. There's no right or wrong, but the answers help determine your child's personality type. Based on the results, K&L places each child into a category based on animal names such as the Owl, the Panda, or the Meerkat.

The character traits associated with each animal reflect the behaviors associated with each creature. For example, the Owl is described as:

> *Curious, self-sufficient and natural problem solvers. They're happiest when given opportunities to figure out how systems work and find solutions to make them better.*

After the test, you'll receive a more in-depth explanation of their personality traits. Since we've started with the Owl, let's keep going. If your child is an Owl, their personality behaviors are:

- *Owls like yourself tend to gain energy by being in your head, with your own thoughts, ideas, dreams, and visions.*
- *You prefer quiet rather than loud.*
- *Owl's tend to make decisions based on logic and facts, and value accuracy in order to solve problems.*
- *You tend to prefer spontaneity and a loosely held schedule because the unplanned and unexpected brings an abundance of joy and excitement.*
- *You tend to be pressure-prompted and will get your best ideas and work done at the last minute.*

If your child is the Owl, we learn a few things right away. They LOVE surprises! Your Owl probably enjoys plenty of quiet time and it's probably best to not schedule out their entire day. Leave some time for them to spend on their own. Let them be spontaneous! And they may prefer to do their schoolwork at the very last minute. This probably drives you a little crazy, but that's when they're at their best.

The K&L quiz offers more in-depth information than presented here. Taking the quiz with the more basic answers is free, but you have the option of buying an eBook on your child's personality type for $12.99 if you really want to dig in deep.

You can find K&L's *Animal Genius Quiz* at https://knowandlove.com/

Myers-Briggs Type Indicator (MBTI)

Parents, you can take K&L's personality quiz as well. It might be fun to compare animal characteristics with your whole family. But if you prefer a more adult-oriented personality test, Myers-Briggs is the current gold standard. If you haven't taken a personality test yourself yet, you really should. I know I learned a great deal about myself from Myers-Briggs.

Seventy years of research found people fall into 16 main personality types. Understanding your personality type helps you understand your strengths and weaknesses, relationships with others, potential career paths, best prospective romantic partners, etc. Instead of animal names, MBTI breaks down personality types into four letter codes. The Owl corresponds with INTP. INTP stands for Introverted, Intuitive, Thinking, and Prospecting. To show you the kind of information you may learn about yourself, let's explore one of the personality types. Since I'm an ESTJ, let's explore that one. I hope I don't bore you too much. Remember, no one personality type is considered superior to the others, except for ESTJ! (just joking).

MBTI identifies ESTJ as the *efficient organizer* (I have my moments).[197] Each letter stands for a character trait. "E" stands for *Extraverted*, which means I like to spend time with others. "S" is for *Sensing*, which means I pay attention to my five senses. "T" equals *Thinking*, so I weigh principles and facts heavily. And "J" stands for *Judging*. From this book, I'm sure you can tell I'm a *big ole judger* alright. But as far as Myers-Briggs is concerned, judging means I prefer a structured lifestyle, which might explain why I spent 22 years in the military.

---

[197] *ESTJ strengths & weaknesses—understanding ESTJ, MBTIonline, The Myers-Briggs Company.* Available at: https://www.mbtionline.com/en-US/MBTI-Types/ESTJ/Strengths-and-weaknesses

Each personality type has strengths and weaknesses. According to *verywellmind.com*, ESTJs are often dependable, hard-working, and self-confident. However, they can also be insensitive, inflexible, and have trouble expressing feelings. Again, no one type is considered better than the others. ESTJs use logic to make decisions instead of feelings. They enjoy investigating things with an immediate, real-world impact (like this book). They often get disinterested in theories and the abstract. ESTJs excel at making fast, decisive choices, but may sometimes rush to judgement. ESTJs are often effective leaders, but they can also be seen as indifferent. As a leader, I have certainly been seen as indifferent in the past, even though that was always very far from the truth. To anyone reading this book, if I were ever your leader and seemed indifferent to you at any time, I profusely apologize.

As far as relationships are concerned, ESTJs take their commitments very seriously. ESTJs tend to be loyal and convey feelings through actions, but can also avoid feelings and emotions, which may be difficult for some partners. ESTJs may shun giving compliments that others like to hear. As extroverts, ESTJs often shine in social situations and enjoy being the center of attention. Perhaps that's why I narrated my audiobook myself. ESTJs place high value on family and put a great deal of effort into fulfilling their obligations to loved ones. On the downside, ESTJs tend to be rigid with rules and routines. They can also ignore advice from others, even when it's good advice.

When it comes to careers, ESTJs appreciate jobs with order and organization. They like ensuring rules and traditions are followed, and they tend to respect authority and accomplish their tasks in a timely manner. Suggested professions include police officer, the military (22 years!), judge (I'm definitely a big ole judger), politician, teacher, business manager, etc.[198]

---

[198]Cherry, K. (2023) *What an ESTJ Myers-Briggs type means for you*, Verywell Mind. Available at: https://www.verywellmind.com/estj-extraverted-sensing-thinking-judging-2795985

Again, if you've never taken a Myers-Briggs-type personality test, I highly endorse it. You can learn a great deal about yourself which will help you become a better parent, make better decisions in your life, and strengthen your relationships with others. At the time of this book writing, Myers-Briggs charges $60 to take their MBTI test,[199] but you can find plenty of free ones on the internet. *16personalities.com* is free and comes highly recommended.[200]

PRIMARY LESSONS: In my opinion, ethnic studies may be the single, most exciting educational instrument for students of color that we've seen in a long time. As the Stanford researchers say, the achievement gap is *"disturbingly large and stubbornly persistent."* However, we've also seen the achievement gap is showing signs of decay. With ethnic studies, we may finally have found a tool with which we can more quickly overcome this achievement gap. Self-study and self-awareness have real value!!!

Unfortunately, CRT supporters have hijacked this precious tool for their own political purposes. They've turned it into a weapon to teach children to hate others based on race. That is the real crime. Even worse, they secretly installed CRT into school curricula and subjects across the country. Perhaps worst of all, they lie to your faces about it and the people they pretend to help are their real victims.

When making an argument against CRT with school officials, use a positive ethnic studies vs. negative ethnic studies model. That assumes the school official isn't completely denying they teach CRT in the first place. Ask them how negative-focused lessons can create positive results? You can always find *something* positive in everything, but CRT's intended *Psychology of Shame* makes it very difficult. And yes, it's all being done on purpose.

---

[199] *Official Myers Briggs test & personality assessment, MBTIonline, The Myers-Briggs Company.* Available at: https://www.mbtionline.com/en-US/

[200] *Free personality test, 16Personalities.* Available at: https://www.16personalities.com/free-personality-test

Conclusion

If the SESR honestly found dramatically positive results for children using critical social engagement, as they claim, think how much more effective ethnic studies could be without the integrated *Psychology of Shame*. Yes, our nation has had its difficulties, but what society hasn't? There is a time and place to teach that part of our history, but K through 6, in particular, is not the time nor the place. Remember, even parents were negatively affected by CRT when investigating their children's school lessons. Don't let them steal your child's innocence. Don't let them turn your child into their next social justice vigilante. Finally, remember, your child's future is up to you, not them.

> *We cannot continue to send our children to Caesar for their education and be surprised when they come home as Romans.*
>
> **Voddie T. Baucham, Jr.**

Printed in the USA
CPSIA information can be obtained
at www.ICGtesting.com
LVHW051452220524
780577LV00009B/799